CAMBRIDGE SCHOOL

Shakespeare

A Midsummer Night's Dream

Edited by Linda Buckle and Paul Kelley

Series Editor: Rex Gibson
Director, Shakespeare and Schools Project

CAMBRIDGE
UNIVERSITY PRESS

£4.95

PUBLISHED BY THE PRESS SYNDICATE OF THE UNIVERSITY OF CAMBRIDGE
The Pitt Building, Trumpington Street, Cambridge, United Kingdom

CAMBRIDGE UNIVERSITY PRESS
The Edinburgh Building, Cambridge CB2 2RU, UK
40 West 20th Street, New York, NY 10011–4211, USA
477 Williamstown Road, Port Melbourne, VIC 3207, Australia
Ruiz de Alarcón 13, 28014 Madrid, Spain
Dock House, The Waterfront, Cape Town 8001, South Africa

http://www.cambridge.org

First published 1992
Revised edition 2000
Seventh printing 2004

Printed in the United Kingdom at the University Press, Cambridge

Typeface Monotype Ehrhardt 11/13pt.   *System* QuarkXPress®

A catalogue record for this book is available from the British Library

Library of Congress Cataloguing in Publication data applied for

ISBN 0 521 78728 9

Prepared for publication by Stenton Associates
Designed by Richard Morris, Stonesfield Design
Picture research by Callie Kendall

Thanks are due to the following for permission to reproduce photographs:

4, 36, 64, 74, 80, 130, 151, Shakespeare Centre Library, Stratford-upon-Avon; 6,
56, Shakespeare Centre Library, Stratford-upon-Avon/Thos. F. and Mig Holte
Collection; 22, 76, 100, 140, Robert Barber; 24, Photo courtesy of the Stratford
Festival Archives/photographer: Zöe Dominic; 30, 88, The New Shakespeare
Company Ltd/photo: John Timbers; 42, Royal Exchange Theatre,
Manchester/photo: John Peters; 44, 66, Shakespeare Centre Library, Stratford-
upon-Avon/photo: David Farrell; 54, 132, BBC Picture Archives; 62, Neil Libbert;
92, 120, Alastair Muir; 98, Edvard Munch: *Geschrei* (*The Scream*), c. 1893
(engraving)/Private Collection/Roger-Viollet/Bridgeman Art Library/©Munch
Museum/Munch-Ellingsen Group, BONO, Oslo, DACS, London 2000; 102, 159,
Donald Cooper/Photostage; 114, 148, Hull Truck Theatre Company/photo: Steve
Morgan; 161, Photograph from *A Midsummer Night's Dream* reprinted with the
permission of Twentieth Century Fox Film Corporation. *A Midsummer Night's
Dream* © 1998, Twentieth Century Fox Film Corporation. All rights reserved.

Contents

Cambridge School Shakespeare

This edition of *A Midsummer Night's Dream* is part of the *Cambridge School Shakespeare* series. Like every other play in the series, it has been specially prepared to help all students in schools and colleges.

This *A Midsummer Night's Dream* aims to be different from other editions of the play. It invites you to bring the play to life in your classroom, hall or drama studio through enjoyable activities that will increase your understanding. Actors have created their different interpretations of the play over the centuries. Similarly, you are encouraged to make up your own mind about *A Midsummer Night's Dream*, rather than having someone else's interpretation handed down to you.

Cambridge School Shakespeare does not offer you a cut-down or simplified version of the play. This is Shakespeare's language, filled with imaginative possibilities. You will find on every left-hand page: a summary of the action, an explanation of unfamiliar words, and a choice of activities on Shakespeare's language, characters and stories.

Between each act and in the pages at the end of the play, you will find notes, illustrations and activities. These will help to increase your understanding of the whole play.

There are a large number of activities to give you the widest choice to suit your own particular needs. Please don't think you have to do every one. Choose the activities that help you most.

This edition will be of value to you whether you are studying for an examination, reading for pleasure, or thinking of putting on the play to entertain others. You can work on the activities on your own or in groups. Many of the activities suggest a particular group size, but don't be afraid to make up smaller or larger groups to suit your own purposes.

Although you are invited to treat *A Midsummer Night's Dream* as a play, you don't need special dramatic or theatrical skills to do the activities. By choosing your activities, and by exploring and experimenting, you can make your own interpretations of Shakespeare's language, characters and stories. Whatever you do, remember that Shakespeare wrote his plays to be acted, watched and enjoyed.

Rex Gibson

This edition of *A Midsummer Night's Dream* uses the text of the play established by R.A. Foakes in *The New Cambridge Shakespeare*.

List of characters

The court

HIPPOLYTA queen of the Amazons, engaged to Theseus
THESEUS duke of Athens, engaged to Hippolyta
EGEUS father of Hermia
PHILOSTRATE master of the revels to the Athenian court

The lovers

HERMIA in love with Lysander
HELENA in love with Demetrius
LYSANDER in love with Hermia
DEMETRIUS Egeus' choice as a husband for Hermia

The Mechanicals
(workers who put on a play)

NICK BOTTOM a weaver who plays Pyramus
PETER QUINCE a carpenter who speaks the Prologue
FRANCIS FLUTE a bellows-mender who plays Thisbe
TOM SNOUT a tinker who plays Wall
ROBIN STARVELING a tailor who plays Moonshine
SNUG a joiner who plays Lion

The fairies

PUCK (or Robin Goodfellow) Oberon's attendant
OBERON king of the fairies
TITANIA queen of the fairies
PEASEBLOSSOM ⎫
COBWEB   ⎬ Titania's fairy attendants
MOTH   ⎪
MUSTARDSEED ⎭
A FAIRY in Titania's service

*Theseus regrets that time is moving slowly before he can marry
Hippolyta. She says the four days will quickly pass.
Theseus orders preparations for their marriage.*

---

1 Theseus and Hippolyta (in pairs)

Shakespeare chooses to use characters from a myth well-known in
his day. In the myth, Theseus, the duke of Athens, fought a battle
with the Amazons (a group of warrior women) and then married
Hippolyta, their queen. Taking parts, read lines 1–19 aloud,
perhaps more than once. Then talk about what sort of relationship
this seems to be.

2 Another angle on the speeches (in pairs)

Identify the key words and images in lines 1–19 and see what
patterns there are (like all those to do with the moon, or 'slow'
versus 'quickly'). These patterns and the relationship between
Theseus and Hippolyta give an idea of what the play will be about.
Try to guess what might happen, and then share your ideas with
another pair.

3 Is there something wrong here? (in groups of four)

Taking parts (with one person as Philostrate and one as director/
audience), walk through this opening, trying to develop gestures
and movements that fit the speeches. Try making one partner
dominant and the other quiet (or even resentful). Have them in
love and affectionate. Discuss which you like best, and why.

4 Moon, night and dreams (in groups of four)

Think about the title of the play and the first speeches. What kind
of dream could this play be (a dream for the characters, or for the
audience, or …)?

---

nuptial hour wedding time
step-dame stepmother
dowager a widow with money or
  property
revenue wealth

steep swallow, absorb
solemnities formal ceremonies
pale companion moon
pomp celebration

A Midsummer Night's Dream

ACT 1   SCENE 1
Athens   Theseus' Palace

Enter THESEUS, HIPPOLYTA, PHILOSTRATE, *with others*

THESEUS Now, fair Hippolyta, our nuptial hour
    Draws on apace; four happy days bring in
    Another moon – but O, methinks, how slow
    This old moon wanes! She lingers my desires,
    Like to a step-dame or a dowager   5
    Long withering out a young man's revenue.
HIPPOLYTA Four days will quickly steep themselves in night;
    Four nights will quickly dream away the time;
    And then the moon, like to a silver bow
    New bent in heaven, shall behold the night   10
    Of our solemnities.
THESEUS   Go, Philostrate,
    Stir up the Athenian youth to merriments,
    Awake the pert and nimble spirit of mirth;
    Turn melancholy forth to funerals;
    The pale companion is not for our pomp.   15
                     [Exit Philostrate]
    Hippolyta, I wooed thee with my sword,
    And won thy love doing thee injuries;
    But I will wed thee in another key,
    With pomp, with triumph, and with revelling.

Egeus enters with his daughter Hermia and the two men who wish to marry her, Lysander (whom she loves) and Demetrius (whom she dislikes). Egeus claims Lysander has 'bewitched' Hermia.

1 Egeus' complaint (in groups of four)

Is Egeus being totally unreasonable, or is he a responsible Athenian father? Let one member of your group be Egeus and the rest a 'court'. Ask 'Egeus' questions and let him explain and defend what he says in lines 22–45.

Hippolyta does not speak during Egeus' 'complaint' or Theseus' response and yet her expression here speaks volumes. What is she thinking? Prepare her thoughts in note form. Then practise these ideas as a monologue. You may like to voice them in character to the class or straight to camera.

feigning untrue, deceitful
gauds, conceits fancy trinkets
Knacks knick-knacks
nosegays posies of flowers

sweetmeats sweets, candies
prevailment pressure
filched stolen

Enter EGEUS *and his daughter* HERMIA, LYSANDER *and* DEMETRIUS

EGEUS Happy be Theseus, our renownèd Duke!   20
THESEUS Thanks, good Egeus. What's the news with thee?
EGEUS Full of vexation come I, with complaint
       Against my child, my daughter Hermia.
       Stand forth, Demetrius! – My noble lord,
       This man hath my consent to marry her.   25
       Stand forth, Lysander! – And, my gracious Duke,
       This man hath bewitched the bosom of my child.
       Thou, thou, Lysander, thou hast given her rhymes,
       And interchanged love-tokens with my child.
       Thou hast by moonlight at her window sung   30
       With feigning voice verses of feigning love,
       And stolen the impression of her fantasy,
       With bracelets of thy hair, rings, gauds, conceits,
       Knacks, trifles, nosegays, sweetmeats – messengers
       Of strong prevailment in unhardened youth;   35
       With cunning hast thou filched my daughter's heart,
       Turned her obedience, which is due to me,
       To stubborn harshness. And, my gracious Duke,
       Be it so she will not here, before your grace,
       Consent to marry with Demetrius,   40
       I beg the ancient privilege of Athens;
       As she is mine, I may dispose of her;
       Which shall be either to this gentleman
       Or to her death, according to our law
       Immediately provided in that case.   45

*Hermia pleads to be allowed to choose Lysander for a husband.
Theseus warns her to abide by Egeus' decision, otherwise she risks
being sent to a convent or to her death.*

Suggest a line as a suitable caption to this picture.

1 Parents versus children (in groups of four to six)

Talk together about what Theseus says opposite, and what children
owe to their parents. Consider the opposite view as well – parents
may be the biggest problem a child has to face as they grow to
being an adult. Draw up a list of advantages and disadvantages of
arranged marriages. Then look again at Hermia's decision: given the
Athenian law, explain what you think of what she decides to do.

imprinted moulded, stamped	**distilled** made into perfume
wanting not having	**unwishèd yoke**
blood feelings	unwanted constraint
mewed confined	**sovereignty** power, control
barren sister nun	

THESEUS What say you, Hermia? Be advised, fair maid.
　　　　To you your father should be as a god,
　　　　One that composed your beauties; yea, and one
　　　　To whom you are but as a form in wax
　　　　By him imprinted, and within his power　　　　　　　　50
　　　　To leave the figure, or disfigure it.
　　　　Demetrius is a worthy gentleman.
HERMIA So is Lysander.
THESEUS 　　　　　　In himself he is;
　　　　But in this kind, wanting your father's voice,
　　　　The other must be held the worthier.　　　　　　　　55
HERMIA I would my father looked but with my eyes.
THESEUS Rather your eyes must with his judgement look.
HERMIA I do entreat your grace to pardon me.
　　　　I know not by what power I am made bold,
　　　　Nor how it may concern my modesty　　　　　　　　60
　　　　In such a presence here to plead my thoughts;
　　　　But I beseech your grace that I may know
　　　　The worst that may befall me in this case,
　　　　If I refuse to wed Demetrius.
THESEUS Either to die the death, or to abjure　　　　　　　　65
　　　　For ever the society of men.
　　　　Therefore, fair Hermia, question your desires,
　　　　Know of your youth, examine well your blood,
　　　　Whether, if you yield not to your father's choice,
　　　　You can endure the livery of a nun,　　　　　　　　70
　　　　For aye to be in shady cloister mewed,
　　　　To live a barren sister all your life,
　　　　Chanting faint hymns to the cold fruitless moon.
　　　　Thrice blessèd they that master so their blood
　　　　To undergo such maiden pilgrimage;　　　　　　　　75
　　　　But earthlier happy is the rose distilled
　　　　Than that which, withering on the virgin thorn,
　　　　Grows, lives, and dies in single blessedness.
HERMIA So will I grow, so live, so die, my lord,
　　　　Ere I will yield my virgin patent up　　　　　　　　80
　　　　Unto his lordship, whose unwishèd yoke
　　　　My soul consents not to give sovereignty.

Theseus orders Hermia to make her decision before his wedding to Hippolyta. Lysander argues his case and points out that Demetrius loved Helena before Hermia.

1 Hermia's dilemma

Would you rather die or be imprisoned than marry someone you disliked? (assume there is no possibility of divorce). Give reasons for your reply.

2 'Looked but with my eyes' (in groups of two to three)

In line 56, Hermia means she wishes that Egeus could 'see' Lysander as she sees him. The people watching 'see' the debates in lines 46–110 very differently. Discuss what each one sees and why.

3 Male dominance (in groups of four to six)

Already there has been a 'forced' engagement. Go through lines 36–110 finding any images that imply male dominance, for example, 'your father should be as a god'. Read the images about males, then those about females and suggest which you find acceptable and which you find offensive.

4 'Love' and 'dote' (in groups of four to six)

From line 46, there is a good deal of talk about feelings. Try to identify these different feelings and explain what they are. Talk together about which characters are sensitive to other's feelings, and which are not.

---

sealing-day wedding day
aye ever
austerity self-control, abstinence
estate unto give to
well-derived
  of a good family and background

well-possessed rich
vantage rich
avouch guarantee, swear
to his head to his face

THESEUS Take time to pause, and by the next new moon,
    The sealing-day betwixt my love and me
    For everlasting bond of fellowship,   85
    Upon that day either prepare to die
    For disobedience to your father's will,
    Or else to wed Demetrius, as he would,
    Or on Diana's altar to protest
    For aye austerity and single life.   90
DEMETRIUS Relent, sweet Hermia; and, Lysander, yield
    Thy crazèd title to my certain right.
LYSANDER You have her father's love, Demetrius;
    Let me have Hermia's – do you marry him.
EGEUS Scornful Lysander, true, he hath my love,   95
    And what is mine my love shall render him;
    And she is mine, and all my right of her
    I do estate unto Demetrius.
LYSANDER I am, my lord, as well-derived as he,
    As well-possessed: my love is more than his, 100
    My fortunes every way as fairly ranked,
    If not with vantage, as Demetrius';
    And, which is more than all these boasts can be,
    I am beloved of beauteous Hermia.
    Why should not I then prosecute my right?   105
    Demetrius, I'll avouch it to his head,
    Made love to Nedar's daughter, Helena,
    And won her soul; and she, sweet lady, dotes,
    Devoutly dotes, dotes in idolatry,
    Upon this spotted and inconstant man.   110

With a final warning to Hermia, Theseus takes Demetrius and Egeus away to talk to them. Left alone, Lysander and Hermia discuss the problems of lovers.

---

1 Hippolyta speaks (in pairs)

Hippolyta remains silent throughout this extremely emotional debate about Hermia. She and Theseus leave together. They will shortly be married. Improvise the conversation they may have about what has just happened, what each thinks of the situation and the characters involved. Bear in mind how Hippolyta might relate to Hermia's plight and Theseus' judgement.

2 Love – 'short as any dream' (in pairs)

In lines 141–9, Lysander paints love as a temporary thing ('momentany', 'swift', 'short', 'brief'), surrounded by a hostile world. Talk about what he compares love to, and whether you think the comparisons are suitable.

3 'The course of true love never did run smooth'

Line 134 has become a commonplace saying. How true is it? Think about what it might be implying about the rest of the play. Which films use this saying as a theme?

4 The dance of the lovers – who loves whom? (I)

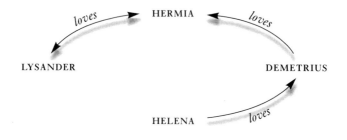

---

extenuate change, reduce	**enthralled** bound
Against in preparation for	**misgraffèd** mismatched
Beteem grant	**collied** darkened, like coal
blood class, family background	**spleen** burst of temper

THESEUS I must confess that I have heard so much,
            And with Demetrius thought to have spoke thereof;
            But, being overfull of self-affairs,
            My mind did lose it. But Demetrius, come,
            And come, Egeus. You shall go with me;   115
            I have some private schooling for you both.
            For you, fair Hermia, look you arm yourself
            To fit your fancies to your father's will;
            Or else the law of Athens yields you up
            (Which by no means we may extenuate)   120
            To death, or to a vow of single life.
            Come, my Hippolyta; what cheer, my love?
            Demetrius and Egeus, go along;
            I must employ you in some business
            Against our nuptial, and confer with you   125
            Of something nearly that concerns yourselves.
EGEUS With duty and desire we follow you.
                            Exeunt all but Lysander and Hermia
LYSANDER How now, my love? Why is your cheek so pale?
            How chance the roses there do fade so fast?
HERMIA Belike for want of rain, which I could well   130
            Beteem them from the tempest of my eyes.
LYSANDER Ay me! For aught that I could ever read,
            Could ever hear by tale or history,
            The course of true love never did run smooth;
            But either it was different in blood –   135
HERMIA O cross! too high to be enthralled to low.
LYSANDER Or else misgraffèd in respect of years –
HERMIA O spite! too old to be engaged to young.
LYSANDER Or else it stood upon the choice of friends –
HERMIA O hell, to choose love by another's eyes!   140
LYSANDER Or, if there were a sympathy in choice,
            War, death, or sickness did lay siege to it,
            Making it momentany as a sound,
            Swift as a shadow, short as any dream,
            Brief as the lightning in the collied night,   145
            That in a spleen unfolds both heaven and earth,
            And, ere a man hath power to say 'Behold!',
            The jaws of darkness do devour it up.
            So quick bright things come to confusion.

Lysander and Hermia plan to elope. They arrange to meet 'tomorrow night' in the wood outside the city.

---

1 Running away (in small groups)

Begin by talking about running away from problems and running away as a couple. Is it ever a wise move? Consider Lysander and Hermia's situation and list the different options the lovers have and which is wisest. Plot a storyboard which presents a modern-day dilemma which could be sorted out by running away.

2 'Teach our trial patience' (in pairs)

Hermia suggests (line 152) that they be patient, and Lysander agrees ('A good persuasion'), but then he suggests they run away. The two lovers (and especially Hermia here) seem to swing from one mood to another. Find a space and act out lines 150–79, trying to emphasise the changing mood of each character by what they do, and how they speak.

3 What 'dream'? (in small groups)

Hermia speaks of features of love ('fancy's followers') like thoughts and wishes and dreams. Talk about what sort of dreams lovers have (being together, freedom from restrictions, happiness, sex ...). She also swears oaths by the goddess of love (Venus) and other lovers (Dido, queen of Carthage who loved Aeneas, the false Trojan). Love, for Hermia, is like a dream she lives in all the time. Is this what love is like? Do you think people in love are inhabiting a dream world?

---

edict command
persuasion doctrine, set of
  principles

revenue wealth
league about three miles
do observance to celebrate

HERMIA If then true lovers have been ever crossed   150
        It stands as an edict in destiny.
        Then let us teach our trial patience,
        Because it is a customary cross,
        As due to love as thoughts, and dreams, and sighs,
        Wishes, and tears – poor fancy's followers.   155
LYSANDER A good persuasion. Therefore hear me, Hermia:
        I have a widow aunt, a dowager,
        Of great revenue, and she hath no child.
        From Athens is her house remote seven leagues;
        And she respects me as her only son.   160
        There, gentle Hermia, may I marry thee;
        And to that place the sharp Athenian law
        Cannot pursue us. If thou lov'st me, then
        Steal forth thy father's house tomorrow night,
        And in the wood, a league without the town   165
        (Where I did meet thee once with Helena
        To do observance to a morn of May),
        There will I stay for thee.
HERMIA   My good Lysander,
        I swear to thee by Cupid's strongest bow,
        By his best arrow with the golden head,   170
        By the simplicity of Venus' doves,
        By that which knitteth souls and prospers loves,
        And by that fire which burned the Carthage queen
        When the false Trojan under sail was seen,
        By all the vows that ever men have broke   175
        (In number more than ever women spoke),
        In that same place thou hast appointed me,
        Tomorrow truly will I meet with thee.
LYSANDER Keep promise, love. Look, here comes Helena.

Helena enters and talks of Demetrius' love for Hermia.
She wishes she were like Hermia. To console her, Hermia and
Lysander tell her of their plan to elope.

1 What do you make of Helena? (in pairs)

Read through Helena and Hermia's lines 180–207, then talk about Helena and her situation. Identify key words and phrases that bring out her character. Read these aloud, or act out the lines emphasising those key words and phrases. What do you feel about Helena?

2 Another fine mess you've got us into, William (in groups of four to six)

Shakespeare seems to have begun his play by setting up an extremely difficult situation for his lovers (remember that Helena is in love too, even if her love is not returned). If the play is a comedy, in the sense that there is a happy ending for all the lovers, it's a bit hard to see how it will happen. Invent a variety of different plots that might bring them together at the end.

3 Looking for patterns (in pairs)

Poetry is a kind of patterned speech or writing. You've probably noticed how the play is in blank verse and rhyming couplets so far (even if you didn't know the name of this kind of poetry). But Shakespeare also uses other patterns. Look at lines 194–201 and see what kinds of patterns you can find in this conversation.

4 'Seemed Athens as a paradise to me'

Hermia says her feelings for Athens have completely changed (line 205). From what you know so far, what kind of place do you think Athens is? How does it compare to the world you live in?

Whither away?
  where are you going?
fair beauty
lodestars guiding star

favour appearance
bated excepted
Phoebe Diana, goddess of the
  moon, associated with chastity

Enter HELENA

HERMIA   God speed, fair Helena! Whither away?   180
HELENA   Call you me fair? That 'fair' again unsay.
          Demetrius loves your fair: O happy fair!
          Your eyes are lodestars, and your tongue's sweet air
          More tuneable than lark to shepherd's ear
          When wheat is green, when hawthorn buds appear.   185
          Sickness is catching. O, were favour so,
          Yours would I catch, fair Hermia, ere I go;
          My ear should catch your voice, my eye your eye,
          My tongue should catch your tongue's sweet melody.
          Were the world mine, Demetrius being bated,   190
          The rest I'd give to be to you translated.
          O, teach me how you look, and with what art
          You sway the motion of Demetrius' heart.
HERMIA   I frown upon him; yet he loves me still.
HELENA   O that your frowns would teach my smiles such skill!   195
HERMIA   I give him curses; yet he gives me love.
HELENA   O that my prayers could such affection move!
HERMIA   The more I hate, the more he follows me.
HELENA   The more I love, the more he hateth me.
HERMIA   His folly, Helena, is no fault of mine.   200
HELENA   None but your beauty; would that fault were mine!
HERMIA   Take comfort: he no more shall see my face;
          Lysander and myself will fly this place.
          Before the time I did Lysander see,
          Seemed Athens as a paradise to me.   205
          O then, what graces in my love do dwell,
          That he hath turned a heaven unto a hell?
LYSANDER Helen, to you our minds we will unfold:
          Tomorrow night, when Phoebe doth behold
          Her silver visage in the watery glass,   210
          Decking with liquid pearl the bladed grass
          (A time that lovers' flights doth still conceal),
          Through Athens' gates have we devised to steal.

Hermia and Lysander leave, wishing Helena luck with Demetrius. Helena reflects on the transforming and deceiving nature of love, and decides to tell Demetrius of the elopement.

1 The lovers (in groups of four)

This scene ends with Helena's decision to tell Demetrius about the elopement, which can only lead to trouble. Discuss the four lovers separately, as they have appeared in this scene, trying to bring out what you think of each. Think in terms of the different relationships (Hermia and Helena, Hermia and Demetrius, and so on). Consider how they are different and how the same, and which you like best (and least).

Work out a typical pose for each character which sums up your perception of them so far, and hold it for other students to guess. Take a photograph if you can.

2 Looking back (in groups of four)

Hermia talks of her past times with Helena ('where often you and I ...'). Imagine what might have occurred in the past two months leading up to this scene – meetings between any of the lovers, incidents, conversations or arguments, and so on. Pick one or two and improvise them. Show your favourite to the class as a whole.

3 Love – Helena's view (in pairs)

Helena explains what she thinks of love in lines 232–9, using a comparison with Cupid (the mythical god of love, a young child with wings, who was sometimes presented as being blind). Work carefully through these lines, two lines at a time, until you're sure of what she's saying (ask for help if you need it). Discuss Helena's view of love. Is it true of lovers you know?

---

were wont used	**waggish** mischievous
holding no quantity	**forswear** falsely promise
having no value	**ere** before
figure suggest	**eyne** eyes
beguiled tricked	**intelligence** information

HERMIA And in the wood, where often you and I
Upon faint primrose beds were wont to lie,   215
Emptying our bosoms of their counsel sweet,
There my Lysander and myself shall meet,
And thence from Athens turn away our eyes
To seek new friends and stranger companies.
Farewell, sweet playfellow; pray thou for us,   220
And good luck grant thee thy Demetrius.
Keep word, Lysander; we must starve our sight
From lovers' food till morrow deep midnight.
LYSANDER I will, my Hermia.

Exit Hermia

Helena, adieu!
As you on him, Demetrius dote on you.   *Exit Lysander* 225
HELENA How happy some o'er other some can be!
Through Athens I am thought as fair as she.
But what of that? Demetrius thinks not so;
He will not know what all but he do know.
And as he errs, doting on Hermia's eyes,   230
So I, admiring of his qualities.
Things base and vile, holding no quantity,
Love can transpose to form and dignity.
Love looks not with the eyes, but with the mind,
And therefore is winged Cupid painted blind.   235
Nor hath love's mind of any judgement taste;
Wings, and no eyes, figure unheedy haste;
And therefore is love said to be a child
Because in choice he is so oft beguiled.
As waggish boys in game themselves forswear,   240
So the boy Love is perjured everywhere;
For, ere Demetrius looked on Hermia's eyne,
He hailed down oaths that he was only mine,
And when this hail some heat from Hermia felt,
So he dissolved, and showers of oaths did melt.   245
I will go tell him of fair Hermia's flight:
Then to the wood will he, tomorrow night,
Pursue her; and for this intelligence,
If I have thanks it is a dear expense;
But herein mean I to enrich my pain,   250
To have his sight thither, and back again.   *Exit*

A group of workers (the Mechanicals) – Quince, Snug, Bottom, Flute, Snout and Starveling – meet to prepare a play for the duke's wedding.

1 Who have we here? (I) (in groups of six)

Shakespeare gives these characters distinctive names and trades. As a group, consider each one in turn, and how the name and trade helps establish their character. Choose a character, and work for a little while on your own, reading your character's lines and thinking about how to develop your part. Come back together to act out this scene. You might like to keep together as a team for the Mechanicals' sections of the play.

2 We've hit Bottom

Everyone knows a Bottom-like character – perhaps there is even one in your group. Talk about what you think of Bottom (and what the other Mechanicals think of him). He is one of the most popular of all Shakespeare's characters, despite his being so completely over-the-top – why might this be? Do you think Shakespeare intended the audience to be laughing with him – or at him?

3 Who have we here? (II) (in groups of six)

The Mechanicals, as a group, are a real contrast with the mythical court of Athens, if only because they are so definitely of Shakespeare's time and place. Talk together about the differences between the court and the workmen, and why Shakespeare might have included the Mechanicals and their very different world.

---

interlude play
lamentable sad, distressing
spread yourselves spread out
condole show grief
Ercles Hercules

to tear a cat in to rant and rave. What kind of acting is Bottom used to, and what kind of play?
Phibbus Phoebus, god of the sun, who was supposed to drive a chariot ('car') through the sky

ACT 1   SCENE 2
Athens

Enter QUINCE the Carpenter, and SNUG the Joiner, and BOTTOM the
Weaver, and FLUTE the Bellows-mender, and SNOUT the Tinker and
STARVELING the Tailor

QUINCE Is all our company here?

BOTTOM You were best to call them generally, man by man, according
to the scrip.

QUINCE Here is the scroll of every man's name which is thought fit
through all Athens to play in our interlude before the Duke and   5
the Duchess on his wedding day at night.

BOTTOM First, good Peter Quince, say what the play treats on; then
read the names of the actors; and so grow to a point.

QUINCE Marry, our play is 'The most lamentable comedy and most
cruel death of Pyramus and Thisbe'.   10

BOTTOM A very good piece of work, I assure you, and a merry. Now,
good Peter Quince, call forth your actors by the scroll. Masters,
spread yourselves.

QUINCE Answer as I call you. Nick Bottom, the weaver?

BOTTOM Ready. Name what part I am for, and proceed.   15

QUINCE You, Nick Bottom, are set down for Pyramus.

BOTTOM What is Pyramus? A lover or a tyrant?

QUINCE A lover that kills himself, most gallant, for love.

BOTTOM That will ask some tears in the true performing of it. If I do
it, let the audience look to their eyes: I will move storms, I will   20
condole, in some measure. To the rest – yet my chief humour is
for a tyrant. I could play Ercles rarely, or a part to tear a cat in,
to make all split:

> The raging rocks
> And shivering shocks   25
> Shall break the locks
>   Of prison gates,
> And Phibbus' car
> Shall shine from far,
> And make and mar   30
>   The foolish Fates.

19

Quince assigns parts to each of the Mechanicals. Bottom is
enthusiastic and volunteers to play two roles, but Quince says no.

---

1 'A monstrous little voice' (in groups of six)

The problem of Flute playing a woman (lines 36–44) is partly solved,
so the Mechanicals believe, by Flute speaking in a high-pitched
voice. Discuss how each of the Mechanicals might speak normally,
and then try out different voices for each (different accents, speed,
and so on). For example, if Bottom is playing the play's hero, how
would he try to talk, and how successful would he be?

2 'Let not me play a woman' (in groups of six)

On Shakespeare's stage, all the actors were male. Prepare and then
act out for the rest of the class this scene (Act 1 Scene 2) in which
the characters are all male, and Act 1 Scene 1, lines 180–224 in
which the characters are female. How do you feel about playing
someone of the opposite sex? What problems does it present? What
opportunities does it provide?

3 The Mechanicals' play (in small groups)

The Mechanicals' play changes a lot before it is finally acted. Using
the description in this scene, improvise – or write and perform –
the play as you think it might have been.

4 Believe a play?

The Mechanicals seem to think that if Bottom played the lion's
part he would frighten the women in the audience (lines 60–3).
What does this tell you about the Mechanicals and how they think
about plays?

5 'These visions did appear'

Look carefully at some of the photographs of the Mechanicals in
various productions (see pages 22, 56 and 114). Explain which
version you like best, and which least, and why.

Ercles' vein Hercules' style   **fitted** cast
small high-pitched

This was lofty. Now name the rest of the players. – This is Ercles'
vein, a tyrant's vein; a lover is more condoling.

QUINCE Francis Flute, the bellows-mender?

FLUTE Here, Peter Quince.   35

QUINCE Flute, you must take Thisbe on you.

FLUTE What is Thisbe? A wandering knight?

QUINCE It is the lady that Pyramus must love.

FLUTE Nay, faith, let not me play a woman: I have a beard coming.

QUINCE That's all one: you shall play it in a mask, and you may speak   40
as small as you will.

BOTTOM And I may hide my face, let me play Thisbe too. I'll speak
in a monstrous little voice: 'Thisne, Thisne!' – 'Ah, Pyramus, my
lover dear; thy Thisbe dear, and lady dear.'

QUINCE No, no; you must play Pyramus; and Flute, you Thisbe.   45

BOTTOM Well, proceed.

QUINCE Robin Starveling, the tailor?

STARVELING Here, Peter Quince.

QUINCE Robin Starveling, you must play Thisbe's mother. Tom Snout,
the tinker?   50

SNOUT Here, Peter Quince.

QUINCE You, Pyramus' father; myself, Thisbe's father; Snug, the
joiner, you the lion's part; and I hope here is a play fitted.

Quince completes the arrangements for the play despite Bottom's interruptions. They plan to meet in the wood 'tomorrow night'.

The Mechanicals (Renaissance Theatre Company, 1990).

1 The Mechanicals' language (in pairs)

The Mechanicals' language is very different from that of the court characters. Make a list of contradictions, mistakes and the silly things they say in Scene 2.

extempore ad lib
proper handsome
French crown bald
(caused by sexually transmitted disease)
con learn

be dogged with company
have people watching
draw a bill of
properties compile a list of props
be perfect
know your lines perfectly

SNUG Have you the lion's part written? Pray you, if it be, give it me; for I am slow of study.   55

QUINCE You may do it extempore; for it is nothing but roaring.

BOTTOM Let me play the lion too. I will roar that I will do any man's heart good to hear me. I will roar that I will make the Duke say 'Let him roar again, let him roar again!'

QUINCE And you should do it too terribly, you would fright the   60
Duchess and the ladies that they would shriek; and that were enough to hang us all.

ALL That would hang us, every mother's son.

BOTTOM I grant you, friends, if you should fright the ladies out of their wits they would have no more discretion but to hang us; but I will   65
aggravate my voice so that I will roar you as gently as any sucking dove. I will roar you and 'twere any nightingale.

QUINCE You can play no part but Pyramus; for Pyramus is a sweet-faced man, a proper man as one shall see in a summer's day, a most lovely, gentlemanlike man: therefore you must needs play Pyramus.   70

BOTTOM Well, I will undertake it. What beard were I best to play it in?

QUINCE Why, what you will.

BOTTOM I will discharge it in either your straw-colour beard, your orange-tawny beard, your purple-in-grain beard, or your French- 75
crown-colour beard, your perfect yellow.

QUINCE Some of your French crowns have no hair at all, and then you will play bare-faced. But, masters, here are your parts, and I am to entreat you, request you, and desire you to con them by tomorrow night, and meet me in the palace wood, a mile without   80
the town, by moonlight; there will we rehearse, for if we meet in the city we shall be dogged with company, and our devices known. In the meantime I will draw a bill of properties, such as our play wants. I pray you, fail me not.

BOTTOM We will meet, and there we may rehearse most obscenely and 85
courageously. Take pains, be perfect: adieu!

QUINCE At the Duke's oak we meet.

BOTTOM Enough; hold, or cut bowstrings.

Exeunt

Looking back at Act I

Activities for groups or individuals

1 Hippolyta

The Hippolyta pictured here is dressed as Queen Elizabeth I who was on the throne when this play was written. Elizabeth once famously said: 'I know I have the body of a weak and feeble woman but I have the heart of a king ...'.

Hippolyta is usually a dominant personage on stage, but she says very little. How do you interpret her character, and how might a reminder of the times in which the play was written help you with that interpretation?

2 Reacting to Egeus

Try different ways to act out the Egeus episode in Scene 1, lines 20–43. Then discuss how relevant Egeus' style of parental authority is today. Improvise the following situation in small groups: parents attempt to enforce a ban on a girlfriend or boyfriend they disapprove of, or an arranged marriage is planned. Talk about Shakespeare's version and your own.

3 Egeus: a bully, or ...? (in pairs)

Egeus can appear as nothing more than an egotistical bully. How can he be played so that he presents a different impression from that? Try out some ideas.

4 Love

A Midsummer Night's Dream is a play very much about love. But what is love? In one of the harsher moments in the play, Egeus describes loves as 'feigning' and 'cunning' (Scene 1, lines 31 and 36). Talk together about 'love' and what you think it is. Identify the problems love can cause and what solutions there might be to these problems. Write down your ideas about love, and record other views of love as you come to them in the play.

5 Word pictures

The words characters speak often create 'word pictures', or images in your imagination. Some phrases can conjure up clear visual pictures in your mind's eye ('Chanting faint hymns to the cold fruitless moon'). Other expressions are more complex and are difficult to visualise ('swift as a shadow, short as any dream'). Like every image on stage, all word images can communicate a great deal to your imaginative understanding of the play. Choose a short passage (such as Scene 1, lines 214–23), and talk together about the images they call up in your mind.

6 Imagery and visual images

A play combines verbal imagery with visual images (for example, the actors' gestures and actions). Sometimes the visual images match the verbal imagery – for example, when Puck says 'I'll put a girdle round about the earth', what gesture might he make to physically express the image?. But because every person watching a play will respond in their own way to what they see and hear, for some people the visual images don't match the words. Pick a short passage from Act 1 and rehearse it. Then act it without words (mime it), and then just read the words aloud. Discuss what you find. Do the words match your 'pictures'?

*A fairy in the service of Titania, queen of the fairies, meets Puck.
Puck explains the conflict over an Indian boy between Oberon,
the king of the fairies, and Titania.*

1 The fairy world (I) (in pairs)

This is yet another world being introduced into the play. Build up
an idea of what sort of world it is by sketching the images from
the fairy's speech (lines 2–17). Compare this world with the world
(or worlds) of the first Act, including similarities such as the love
conflict.

2 The fairy world (II) (in pairs)

Act out lines 1–31, working on the gestures and movements that
bring out the world of fairies as you think it should be. Compare
and contrast these characters with the Mechanicals, and with the
Athenian court.

3 What does the audience see? (in groups of four)

Both speeches opposite create visions (or dreams) in the audience's
mind of things that happen in the fairy world. Some images would
be very difficult to put on a stage (for example, 'elves for
fear/Creep into acorn cups'). Discuss how much help the audience
needs to imagine what is described (this scene is set at night in a
wood). You could be like the Mechanicals – very literal in trying
to present everything – or leave it all to the power of Shakespeare's
language.

---

thorough through
orbs fairy rings
savours scent
lob lout
anon soon

passing ... wrath
  very fierce and angry
changeling
  a child stolen by fairies
starlight sheen shining starlight
square quarrel

ACT 2 SCENE 1
The wood

Enter a FAIRY *at one door, and* PUCK, *or* ROBIN GOODFELLOW
at another

PUCK How now, spirit; whither wander you?
FAIRY   Over hill, over dale,
          Thorough bush, thorough briar,
       Over park, over pale,
          Thorough flood, thorough fire;   5
       I do wander everywhere
       Swifter than the moon's sphere;
       And I serve the Fairy Queen,
       To dew her orbs upon the green.
       The cowslips tall her pensioners be;   10
       In their gold coats spots you see –
       Those be rubies, fairy favours,
       In those freckles live their savours.
          I must go seek some dewdrops here,
          And hang a pearl in every cowslip's ear.   15
     Farewell, thou lob of spirits; I'll be gone.
     Our Queen and all her elves come here anon.
PUCK The King doth keep his revels here tonight.
     Take heed the Queen come not within his sight,
     For Oberon is passing fell and wrath,   20
     Because that she as her attendant hath
     A lovely boy stol'n from an Indian king;
     She never had so sweet a changeling,
     And jealous Oberon would have the child
     Knight of his train, to trace the forests wild.   25
     But she perforce withholds the lovèd boy,
     Crowns him with flowers, and makes him all her joy.
     And now they never meet in grove or green,
     By fountain clear or spangled starlight sheen,
     But they do square, that all their elves for fear   30
     Creep into acorn cups and hide them there.

Puck and the fairy talk about the sort of 'sprite' Puck is.
In both descriptions he is mischievous and plays tricks.

---

1 Puck: what is he like?

Puck is one of Shakespeare's best-known characters, and both speeches serve to introduce him to the audience. Make a list of the adjectives used to describe him ('shrewd', and so on), and a list of what he is described as doing. Using both lists, describe what kind of character he is. Add to your lists as you continue reading.

2 Speech and actions (in pairs)

Take turns reading Puck's speech (lines 43–58) and fit actions to it, miming some of the things he talks about.

3 What do you see? (in groups of three to four)

Look at the presentations of Puck on pages 36, 42, 74 and 148. Discuss each one, commenting on why Puck looks the way he does. Do any surprise you?

4 Just to think about

This quotation comes from a book Shakespeare probably read called *The Discovery of Witchcraft* (it was written in 1584):

> 'Indeed your grandams' maids set a bowl of milk out for Robin
> Goodfellow ... the mare, the man in the oak, the puckle, hobgoblin.'

The book also describes incidents similar to those the fairy and Puck talk about, but, as the quotation implies, the author said hardly anyone believed in Puck or Robin Goodfellow any more. Why does Shakespeare use so many imaginary characters from myth and superstition in the play?

---

shrewd evil or mischievous. Which do you think suits him best: this or Puck's own description of himself?
knavish roguish, unprincipled
Skim milk skim off the cream
quern hand mill for grinding corn
bootless pointless
barm the head on beer
crab crab apple
dewlap hanging, loose skin on the neck
loffe laugh

FAIRY Either I mistake your shape and making quite,
　　　　Or else you are that shrewd and knavish sprite
　　　　Called Robin Goodfellow. Are not you he
　　　　That frights the maidens of the villagery,　　　　　　　35
　　　　Skim milk, and sometimes labour in the quern,
　　　　And bootless make the breathless housewife churn,
　　　　And sometime make the drink to bear no barm,
　　　　Mislead night-wanderers, laughing at their harm?
　　　　Those that 'Hobgoblin' call you, and 'Sweet Puck',　　　40
　　　　You do their work, and they shall have good luck.
　　　　Are not you he?
PUCK　　　　　　　　Thou speakest aright;
　　　　I am that merry wanderer of the night.
　　　　I jest to Oberon, and make him smile
　　　　When I a fat and bean-fed horse beguile,　　　　　　45
　　　　Neighing in likeness of a filly foal;
　　　　And sometime lurk I in a gossip's bowl
　　　　In very likeness of a roasted crab,
　　　　And when she drinks, against her lips I bob,
　　　　And on her withered dewlap pour the ale.　　　　　50
　　　　The wisest aunt, telling the saddest tale,
　　　　Sometime for threefoot stool mistaketh me;
　　　　Then slip I from her bum, down topples she,
　　　　And 'Tailor' cries, and falls into a cough;
　　　　And then the whole choir hold their hips and loffe,　　55
　　　　And waxen in their mirth, and neeze, and swear
　　　　A merrier hour was never wasted there.
　　　　But room, Fairy: here comes Oberon.
FAIRY And here my mistress. Would that he were gone!

Oberon and Titania enter with their attendants.
They accuse each other of being attracted to the mortals,
Theseus and Hippolyta.

In many ways, what a play looks like is as important as what is said. Discuss what this photograph says ('what's going on?' is a good starting point). Compare it with other photographs of the fairies on pages 42, 44, 66 and 151.

train attendants	**buskined** wearing hunting boots
Tarry wait	**Perigenia, Aegles, Ariadne,**
lord, lady	**Antiopa** women Theseus slept
(they are husband and wife)	with
Corin, Phillida	
two mythical lovers	

Enter OBERON *the King of Fairies, at one door, with his train; and*
TITANIA, *the Queen, at another with hers*

OBERON   Ill met by moonlight, proud Titania!   60
TITANIA   What, jealous Oberon? Fairies, skip hence.
    I have forsworn his bed and company.
OBERON   Tarry, rash wanton! Am not I thy lord?
TITANIA   Then I must be thy lady. But I know
    When thou hast stol'n away from Fairyland,   65
    And in the shape of Corin sat all day
    Playing on pipes of corn, and versing love
    To amorous Phillida. Why art thou here
    Come from the farthest step of India? –
    But that, forsooth, the bouncing Amazon,   70
    Your buskined mistress and your warrior love,
    To Theseus must be wedded; and you come
    To give their bed joy and prosperity.
OBERON   How canst thou thus, for shame, Titania,
    Glance at my credit with Hippolyta,   75
    Knowing I know thy love to Theseus?
    Didst not thou lead him through the glimmering night
    From Perigenia, whom he ravishèd,
    And make him with fair Aegles break his faith,
    With Ariadne, and Antiopa?   80

Titania claims that the dispute with Oberon has changed the natural patterns of the climate and the seasons.

1 Watch your language (in pairs or groups of three)

Our world is always changing, and so is our language. You can see some of these changes by comparing Shakespeare's language with the way we speak and write today. Use Titania's lines 81–117 to look for evidence of an older way of life ('ox … stretched his yoke') or belief ('Contagious fogs'). You can see how writing about an older way of life naturally means using different language. Then identify words no longer used today. Finally, look for uses of language that are distinctive because this is poetry. Titania describes the disruption of the natural world because of the conflict between her and Oberon (this says something about their power in and over nature). Write another speech (in prose or in verse) about a similar problem of today – global warming. Compare your use of language with Shakespeare's.

2 The relationship (in groups of four to six)

Discuss the relationship between Titania and Oberon as shown in lines 60–117, and the sexual nature of their conversation. This is another conflict between lovers. Talk together about any parallels with the relationships in the first Act, and what sort of mood it creates in the play here. Then discuss the last lines of Titania's speech in lines 115–17, and what they imply about the importance of Oberon and Titania's relationship.

3 Updating 'forgeries of jealousy'

On page 55, you can find an activity on updating Titania's 'forgeries of jealousy' speech

---

forgeries lies
beachèd margent shore
ringlets dancing in a circle
brawls quarrels
murrion flock diseased sheep
nine-men's-morris outdoor game
 (like draughts)

distemperature disorder
old Hiems winter
childing pregnant, fruitful
mazèd amazed, confused: a word
 used frequently in the play
progeny offspring
dissension disagreement

TITANIA These are the forgeries of jealousy:
         And never since the middle summer's spring
         Met we on hill, in dale, forest, or mead,
         By pavèd fountain or by rushy brook,
         Or in the beachèd margent of the sea   85
         To dance our ringlets to the whistling wind,
         But with thy brawls thou hast disturbed our sport.
         Therefore the winds, piping to us in vain,
         As in revenge have sucked up from the sea
         Contagious fogs; which, falling in the land,   90
         Hath every pelting river made so proud
         That they have overborne their continents.
         The ox hath therefore stretched his yoke in vain,
         The ploughman lost his sweat, and the green corn
         Hath rotted ere his youth attained a beard.   95
         The fold stands empty in the drownèd field,
         And crows are fatted with the murrion flock;
         The nine-men's-morris is filled up with mud,
         And the quaint mazes in the wanton green
         For lack of tread are undistinguishable.   100
         The human mortals want their winter cheer;
         No night is now with hymn or carol blessed.
         Therefore the moon, the governess of floods,
         Pale in her anger, washes all the air,
         That rheumatic diseases do abound;   105
         And thorough this distemperature we see
         The seasons alter; hoary-headed frosts
         Fall in the fresh lap of the crimson rose,
         And on old Hiems' thin and icy crown
         An odorous chaplet of sweet summer buds   110
         Is, as in mockery, set. The spring, the summer,
         The childing autumn, angry winter change
         Their wonted liveries, and the mazèd world
         By their increase now knows not which is which.
         And this same progeny of evils comes   115
         From our debate, from our dissension.
         We are their parents and original.

Oberon asks Titania to give up her 'changeling boy', the subject of the quarrel. She explains why she is going to keep him, and Oberon promises to be revenged.

1 Titania refuses a male command (in groups of four)

Look carefully at Titania's reasons for keeping the boy (lines 123–37). Once again in the play, a male is trying to dominate a female – where do your sympathies lie? What kind of character is Titania – or isn't it helpful to view her in this mortal way?

2 Cut it out (in pairs)

Shakespeare's plays are often cut for performance (that is, shortened by leaving some lines or speeches out). Take parts and read lines 118–47 aloud, and then speak them again leaving out lines 123–37. What difference does leaving out these lines make?

List what is gained against what is lost and make an editorial decision about what to do in your production of this episode.

3 Hippolyta, Theseus, Oberon and Titania (in groups of four)

Each person take one role. In role, discuss your situation, your relationships and your problems. Question each other on what you are thinking and feeling. Try to find some common ground. Maybe you could suggest solutions to each other's problems.

---

henchman page
votress member of religious order, worshipper
embarkèd traders
traders who had set sail
wanton mischievous, immoral

swimming gait gliding movement
Perchance maybe
spare avoid
chide downright argue

OBERON Do you amend it, then: it lies in you.
Why should Titania cross her Oberon?
I do but beg a little changeling boy   120
To be my henchman.
TITANIA   Set your heart at rest.
The fairy land buys not the child of me.
His mother was a votress of my order,
And in the spicèd Indian air by night
Full often hath she gossiped by my side,   125
And sat with me on Neptune's yellow sands
Marking th'embarkèd traders on the flood,
When we have laughed to see the sails conceive
And grow big-bellied with the wanton wind;
Which she, with pretty and with swimming gait   130
Following (her womb then rich with my young squire),
Would imitate, and sail upon the land
To fetch me trifles, and return again
As from a voyage, rich with merchandise.
But she, being mortal, of that boy did die,   135
And for her sake do I rear up her boy;
And for her sake I will not part with him.
OBERON How long within this wood intend you stay?
TITANIA Perchance till after Theseus' wedding day.
If you will patiently dance in our round,   140
And see our moonlight revels, go with us:
If not, shun me, and I will spare your haunts.
OBERON Give me that boy, and I will go with thee.
TITANIA Not for thy fairy kingdom! Fairies, away.
We shall chide downright if I longer stay.   145
                    Exeunt [Titania and her train]
OBERON Well, go thy way. Thou shalt not from this grove
Till I torment thee for this injury.

Oberon tells Puck to fetch him 'love-in-idleness' (a flower touched by Cupid's arrow). When the juice of the flower is put on the eyelids of the sleeping, it makes them fall in love with whatever they see when they awake.

1 Words and actions (in pairs)

The director has asked you to choreograph a pacey and action-packed presentation of Oberon's speech and fit actions to the words. Work out a series of actions for both Oberon and Puck and present your performance.

Since when
dulcet soothing, quiet
spheres orbits
vestal virgin (Queen Elizabeth I?)
Cupid's fiery shaft
  Cupid's arrow which was supposed
  to make the person hit fall in love

imperial votress
  (Queen Elizabeth I?)
bolt arrow
leviathan whale

My gentle Puck, come hither. Thou rememberest
Since once I sat upon a promontory,
And heard a mermaid on a dolphin's back   150
Uttering such dulcet and harmonious breath
That the rude sea grew civil at her song,
And certain stars shot madly from their spheres
To hear the sea-maid's music?

PUCK   I remember.

OBERON   That very time I saw (but thou couldst not)   155
Flying between the cold moon and the earth
Cupid all armed: a certain aim he took
At a fair vestal thronèd by the west,
And loosed his loveshaft smartly from his bow
As it should pierce a hundred thousand hearts;   160
But I might see young Cupid's fiery shaft
Quenched in the chaste beams of the watery moon;
And the imperial votress passèd on
In maiden meditation, fancy-free.
Yet marked I where the bolt of Cupid fell: 165
It fell upon a little western flower,
Before, milk-white; now purple with love's wound:
And maidens call it 'love-in-idleness'.
Fetch me that flower, the herb I showed thee once;
The juice of it on sleeping eyelids laid   170
Will make or man or woman madly dote
Upon the next live creature that it sees.
Fetch me this herb, and be thou here again
Ere the leviathan can swim a league.

PUCK   I'll put a girdle round about the earth   175
In forty minutes!   [*Exit*]

37

Oberon plans to use the flower's juice on Titania, then makes himself invisible as Demetrius and Helena enter, arguing. He is looking for Hermia, and Helena has followed him.

1 Oberon's revenge (in pairs)

Read aloud Oberon's lines 176–85, and then consider whether he is fair in doing this. Are you beginning to form an opinion of this character? If he were human, what would you think of him?

2 The argument (I) (in pairs)

Lines 188–213 are very enjoyable to act out, but read them aloud first. Shakespeare was very fond of wordplay (especially in his early comedies), and this is a good example. Look at the patterns of words, and identify some of the different kinds of wordplay here. Read it again, emphasising this wordplay. Would you want to use the wordplay to make this a funny or a cruel scene?

3 The argument (II) (in pairs)

Read through the argument again, thinking about what the characters are feeling – like Titania and Oberon, they are upset and angry. What do you think about the image of being Demetrius' dog that Helena uses? Try reading it to emphasise these feelings.

Now get up and act out the argument, perhaps in different ways, stressing the feelings, or the silliness of it all.

4 The fairy and mortal worlds (in groups of four to six)

Oberon is 'invisible' to the mortals. This – and what has gone before – suggest the extent of his powers. So far, what have you learnt about his powers? Discuss what sort of a relationship there is between the world of the mortals and that of the fairies.

---

wood mad, insane while he is in a real wood. Elizabethans were fond of wordplay and puns, as this episode shows

adamant hard stone, diamond
Leave you give up

OBERON   Having once this juice
       I'll watch Titania when she is asleep,
       And drop the liquor of it in her eyes:
       The next thing then she, waking, looks upon –
       Be it on lion, bear, or wolf, or bull,   180
       On meddling monkey, or on busy ape –
       She shall pursue it with the soul of love.
       And ere I take this charm from off her sight
       (As I can take it with another herb)
       I'll make her render up her page to me.   185
       But who comes here? I am invisible,
       And I will overhear their conference.

          Enter DEMETRIUS, HELENA *following him*

DEMETRIUS I love thee not, therefore pursue me not.
       Where is Lysander, and fair Hermia?
       The one I'll slay, the other slayeth me.   190
       Thou told'st me they were stol'n unto this wood,
       And here am I, and wood within this wood
       Because I cannot meet my Hermia.
       Hence, get thee gone, and follow me no more.
HELENA You draw me, you hard-hearted adamant!   195
       But yet you draw not iron, for my heart
       Is true as steel. Leave you your power to draw,
       And I shall have no power to follow you.
DEMETRIUS Do I entice you? Do I speak you fair?
       Or rather do I not in plainest truth   200
       Tell you I do not, nor I cannot love you?
HELENA And even for that do I love you the more.
       I am your spaniel; and, Demetrius,
       The more you beat me I will fawn on you.
       Use me but as your spaniel: spurn me, strike me,   205
       Neglect me, lose me; only give me leave,
       Unworthy as I am, to follow you.
       What worser place can I beg in your love
       (And yet a place of high respect with me)
       Than to be usèd as you use your dog?   210
DEMETRIUS Tempt not too much the hatred of my spirit;
       For I am sick when I do look on thee.
HELENA And I am sick when I look not on you.

Helena continues to woo Demetrius. He is angry and frustrated at her persistence, and eventually he runs off. She follows him.

---

1 Reclaim the night – the physical threat

Read Demetrius' lines 214–19 as menacingly as you can, and think carefully about the implications of his threat. Women often feel more vulnerable at night, especially in places like a wood. The problem of women's safety at night was obviously real in Shakespeare's day. Discuss whether there are solutions. This way of reading the speech adds a contemporary relevance to the play.

2 Reclaim the night – the moral threat

However, Shakespeare may not have been considering Helena's physical safety as much as the threat to her reputation and respectability. Either way, it adds an unpleasantly hard edge to what is surely a light-hearted play. What other 'hard edges' have you noticed so far in the play?

3 Anything Shakespeare can do, I can do

Helena's couplet at the end (the two rhyming lines 243–4) sums up her feelings. Write a couplet for Demetrius to say to Helena just before he leaves that sums up *his* feelings.

---

impeach call into question
desert lonely, deserted
brakes undergrowth, thicket
griffin beast, half eagle/half lion

hind deer
bootless useless
stay endure
upon by means of

DEMETRIUS You do impeach your modesty too much,
   To leave the city and commit yourself   215
   Into the hands of one that loves you not;
   To trust the opportunity of night,
   And the ill counsel of a desert place,
   With the rich worth of your virginity.
HELENA Your virtue is my privilege: for that   220
   It is not night when I do see your face,
   Therefore I think I am not in the night;
   Nor doth this wood lack worlds of company,
   For you, in my respect, are all the world.
   Then how can it be said I am alone   225
   When all the world is here to look on me?
DEMETRIUS I'll run from thee and hide me in the brakes,
   And leave thee to the mercy of wild beasts.
HELENA The wildest hath not such a heart as you.
   Run when you will: the story shall be changed;   230
   Apollo flies, and Daphne holds the chase,
   The dove pursues the griffin, the mild hind
   Makes speed to catch the tiger – bootless speed,
   When cowardice pursues, and valour flies!
DEMETRIUS I will not stay thy questions. Let me go;   235
   Or if thou follow me, do not believe
   But I shall do thee mischief in the wood.
HELENA Ay, in the temple, in the town, the field,
   You do me mischief. Fie, Demetrius,
   Your wrongs do set a scandal on my sex!   240
   We cannot fight for love, as men may do;
   We should be wooed, and were not made to woo.
              [*Exit Demetrius*]
   I'll follow thee, and make a heaven of hell,
   To die upon the hand I love so well.   *Exit*

Oberon vows to help Helena. Puck returns with the flower. Oberon will use it on Titania when she is asleep. He tells Puck to drop the juice of it in Demetrius' eyes when Helena is near.

1 Out of this world

What impression of the fairies do you gain from the photograph of Puck and Oberon above? How do you think this Oberon would speak lines 248–67? Try out your version of the lines, then speak them in the style of the Oberon shown on page 30 and on page 92.

nymph beautiful woodland
  creature
sometime of during
Weed cloth

OBERON Fare thee well, nymph. Ere he do leave this grove   245
          Thou shalt fly him, and he shall seek thy love.

                    Enter PUCK

          Hast thou the flower there? Welcome, wanderer.
PUCK Ay, there it is.
OBERON   I pray thee give it me.
          I know a bank where the wild thyme blows,
          Where oxlips and the nodding violet grows,   250
          Quite overcanopied with luscious woodbine,
          With sweet musk-roses, and with eglantine:
          There sleeps Titania sometime of the night,
          Lulled in these flowers with dances and delight;
          And there the snake throws her enamelled skin,   255
          Weed wide enough to wrap a fairy in;
          And with the juice of this I'll streak her eyes,
          And make her full of hateful fantasies.
          Take thou some of it, and seek through this grove:
          A sweet Athenian lady is in love   260
          With a disdainful youth; anoint his eyes,
          But do it when the next thing he espies
          May be the lady. Thou shalt know the man
          By the Athenian garments he hath on.
          Effect it with some care, that he may prove   265
          More fond on her than she upon her love.
          And look thou meet me ere the first cock crow.
PUCK Fear not, my lord; your servant shall do so.
                                              Exeunt

Titania orders the fairies to sing her to sleep – and they do.
A single fairy is left to guard the sleeping Titania.

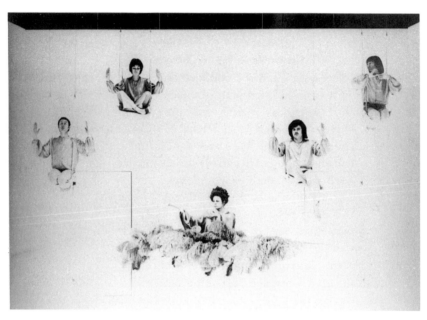

This is how the Royal Shakespeare Company presented Titania and the fairies in 1970. Think about the variety of ways in which you could stage them (body position, facial expression, and so on). Create a variety of tableaux ('frozen moments'), and photograph them, if possible. If you have the resources, experiment with make-up and costumes.

roundel a dance in a circle
cankers caterpillars
reremice bats

offices jobs
double tongue forked tongue
Philomel nightingale

ACT 2   SCENE 2
The wood

Enter TITANIA, *Queen of Fairies, with her train*

TITANIA Come, now a roundel and a fairy song,
        Then for the third part of a minute, hence –
        Some to kill cankers in the musk-rose buds,
        Some war with reremice for their leathern wings
        To make my small elves coats, and some keep back   5
        The clamorous owl that nightly hoots and wonders
        At our quaint spirits. Sing me now asleep;
        Then to your offices, and let me rest.
                      Fairies sing.

[FIRST FAIRY] You spotted snakes with double tongue,
          Thorny hedgehogs, be not seen.   10
        Newts and blindworms, do no wrong,
          Come not near our Fairy Queen.
[CHORUS]   Philomel with melody
          Sing in our sweet lullaby,
        Lulla, lulla, lullaby; lulla, lulla, lullaby.   15
          Never harm
          Nor spell nor charm
          Come our lovely lady nigh.
          So good night, with lullaby.
FIRST FAIRY Weaving spiders, come not here;   20
          Hence, you longlegged spinners, hence!
          Beetles black approach not near;
          Worm nor snail, do no offence.
[CHORUS]   Philomel with melody
          Sing in our sweet lullaby,
                      25
        Lulla, lulla, lullaby; lulla, lulla, lullaby.
          Never harm
          Nor spell nor charm
          Come our lovely lady nigh.
          So good night, with lullaby.   *Titania sleeps.* 30
SECOND FAIRY
          Hence, away! Now all is well;
          One aloof stand sentinel!   *[Exeunt Fairies]*

Oberon puts the flower's juice on Titania's eyes with a charm that she will wake 'when some vile thing is near!'. Lysander and Hermia enter, lost. She rejects his advances and they prepare to sleep.

1 Vile thing, you make my heart sing
(in groups of three)

Read Oberon's lines 33–40 and discuss the idea of wanting your partner to be in love with an animal.

2 Contrast the kinds of love (in groups of three)

Taking parts, read lines 33–67 aloud, and then talk together about the different kinds of love shown here (Oberon's, Lysander's and Hermia's).

3 Just a thought: irony

Line 67 is ironic (since Lysander's love alters in a few minutes, thanks to Puck putting the flower's juice on his eyes instead of Demetrius'). As you read on, look out for other ironies in what people say or do.

4 Change in morality? (in small groups)

Hermia refuses to let Lysander sleep beside her, saying 'Such separation as may well be said/Becomes a virtuous bachelor and a maid.' Have morals changed in the last 400 years? In what ways? And for the better?

languish droop, pine for	**tarry** wait
ounce lynx	**troth** truth
Pard leopard	**much beshrew** a curse upon

Enter OBERON; [*he squeezes the juice on Titania's eyes*]

OBERON   What thou seest when thou dost wake,
          Do it for thy true love take;
          Love and languish for his sake.   35
          Be it ounce or cat or bear,
          Pard, or boar with bristled hair
          In thy eye that shall appear
          When thou wak'st, it is thy dear.
          Wake when some vile thing is near!   [*Exit*]   40

Enter LYSANDER *and* HERMIA

LYSANDER Fair love, you faint with wandering in the wood,
          And, to speak truth, I have forgot our way.
          We'll rest us, Hermia, if you think it good,
          And tarry for the comfort of the day.
HERMIA   Be it so, Lysander; find you out a bed,   45
          For I upon this bank will rest my head.
LYSANDER One turf shall serve as pillow for us both;
          One heart, one bed, two bosoms, and one troth.
HERMIA   Nay, good Lysander, for my sake, my dear,
          Lie further off yet; do not lie so near.   50
LYSANDER O take the sense, sweet, of my innocence!
          Love takes the meaning in love's conference;
          I mean that my heart unto yours is knit,
          So that but one heart we can make of it:
          Two bosoms interchainèd with an oath,   55
          So then two bosoms and a single troth.
          Then by your side no bed-room me deny,
          For lying so, Hermia, I do not lie.
HERMIA   Lysander riddles very prettily.
          Now much beshrew my manners and my pride   60
          If Hermia meant to say Lysander lied.
          But, gentle friend, for love and courtesy
          Lie further off, in human modesty;
          Such separation as may well be said
          Becomes a virtuous bachelor and a maid,   65
          So far be distant, and good night, sweet friend;
          Thy love ne'er alter till thy sweet life end!

Hermia and Lysander sleep, and Puck mistakenly puts the juice in Lysander's eyes. Demetrius enters, chased still by Helena. He quickly leaves again, on his own, into the woods.

1 Young love

Write the thoughts and feelings of Hermia and Lysander as they drift off to sleep. What are they individually thinking about: what has happened so far, the difference of opinion they have just had, or their plans and hopes for the future? Try writing in rhyming couplets as Shakespeare does here.

2 The fairy touch (in pairs)

In this scene, the fairy world, through Puck, directly manipulates the feelings of a mortal. The consequences of such influence could be disturbing. How would you want Puck to approach this?

With one person as Puck and the other as director, act out Puck's speech focusing on his attitude to the mortal whose life he is changing. Try to create a different attitude from Puck, perhaps swapping roles.

3 Emphasise the rhymes? (in pairs)

There are over 700 rhyming lines in this play. Do you think these should be emphasised, or should actors try to stress the syntax – letting lines 'run on' and not drawing attention to the rhymes? Try both approaches with the speeches on the opposite page.

---

approve put to the proof
Weeds clothes
Churl heartless rogue

owe possess
darkling sad, downcast

LYSANDER Amen, amen, to that fair prayer say I,
          And then end life when I end loyalty!
          Here is my bed; sleep give thee all his rest.   70
HERMIA With half that wish the wisher's eyes be pressed.
                    They sleep.

                    Enter PUCK

PUCK   Through the forest have I gone,
              But Athenian found I none
              On whose eyes I might approve
              This flower's force in stirring love.   75
              Night and silence – Who is here?
              Weeds of Athens he doth wear:
              This is he my master said
              Despisèd the Athenian maid;
              And here the maiden, sleeping sound   80
              On the dank and dirty ground.
              Pretty soul, she durst not lie
              Near this lack-love, this kill-courtesy.
              Churl, upon thy eyes I throw
              All the power this charm doth owe.   85
              [*He squeezes the juice on Lysander's eyes.*]
              When thou wak'st let love forbid
              Sleep his seat on thy eyelid.
              So, awake when I am gone;
              For I must now to Oberon.   *Exit*

                    Enter DEMETRIUS *and* HELENA, *running*

HELENA Stay, though thou kill me, sweet Demetrius!   90
DEMETRIUS I charge thee, hence, and do not haunt me thus.
HELENA O wilt thou darkling leave me? Do not so!
DEMETRIUS Stay, on thy peril; I alone will go.   *Exit*

49

Helena stops to rest and sees Lysander.
He wakes up, and immediately falls in love with Helena
because of the flower's magic.

1 Shall I compare me to a bear?

Read through Helena's speech about her own appearance (lines 94–108). Why might she feel this way about herself?

2 Lysander – or not Lysander? (in groups of three)

> 'Lysander gets taken over when he's under the influence of magic; that's where character tends to disappear. It brings out all this raw passion.'

An actor, James Larkin, who played Lysander said this. Try various ways of presenting a transformed Lysander. Share ideas with other groups, and discuss the results and implications.

3 What to make of him (in pairs)

The audience knows that Lysander's 'love' is just magic, but for Helena the Athenian world of conventions and normality must seem far away. Line 109 is often played as farce. Work out how you would perform it to bring out what Helena thinks of Lysander's sudden transformation.

4 The dance of lovers – who loves whom? (II)

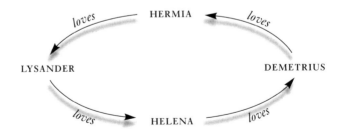

---

fond foolish
dissembling concealing, disguising
glass mirror
sphery eyne star-like eyes

Transparent honest, open
ripe mature
touching reaching

HELENA O, I am out of breath in this fond chase!
           The more my prayer, the lesser is my grace.   95
           Happy is Hermia, wheresoe'er she lies,
           For she hath blessèd and attractive eyes.
           How came her eyes so bright? Not with salt tears –
           If so, my eyes are oftener washed than hers.
           No, no, I am as ugly as a bear,   100
           For beasts that meet me run away for fear.
           Therefore no marvel though Demetrius
           Do as a monster fly my presence thus.
           What wicked and dissembling glass of mine
           Made me compare with Hermia's sphery eyne?   105
           But who is here? – Lysander, on the ground?
           Dead, or asleep? I see no blood, no wound.
           Lysander, if you live, good sir, awake!
LYSANDER [*Waking.*]
           And run through fire I will for thy sweet sake!
           Transparent Helena, nature shows art   110
           That through thy bosom makes me see thy heart.
           Where is Demetrius? O, how fit a word
           Is that vile name to perish on my sword!
HELENA Do not say so, Lysander, say not so.
           What though he love your Hermia? Lord, what though? 115
           Yet Hermia still loves you; then be content.
LYSANDER Content with Hermia? No; I do repent
           The tedious minutes I with her have spent.
           Not Hermia, but Helena I love.
           Who will not change a raven for a dove?   120
           The will of man is by his reason swayed,
           And reason says you are the worthier maid.
           Things growing are not ripe until their season;
           So I, being young, till now ripe not to reason.
           And touching now the point of human skill,   125
           Reason becomes the marshal to my will.
           And leads me to your eyes, where I o'erlook
           Love's stories written in love's richest book.

Helena thinks Lysander is making fun of her, and leaves.
He follows, leaving Hermia behind, still asleep. Hermia wakes from a
nightmare, realises she is alone and goes to find Lysander.

1 What means this dream? (in groups of three)

Talk together about what Hermia's dream might mean.

2 Babes in a wood (in groups of three)

There are three characters, three moods and three different 'dreams' of what is happening here. None of the three characters really understands what is going on. Each choose a character and read their speech aloud, and describe the character's mood and 'dream' of what is happening.

3 Men and women (in groups of three)

Compare the two women's speeches opposite, and see if there are any similarities. Then contrast them with Lysander's. If you find differences between the male and female speeches, share them with the whole class and discuss the implications.

4 Absolute confusion? (in groups of three)

Remind yourselves of the 'dance' of the lovers on page 50 – things couldn't get worse. Find as many negative/upsetting images as you can in lines 129–62. Read aloud just those images and talk together about whether you think that the midsummer night's dream is becoming a nightmare.

5 'Seemed Athens as a paradise to me' (in groups of three)

Hermia entered the wood with high hopes. Compare the world she finds herself in now (the wood, the night, the magic) with the one she left behind.

---

keen	sharp	**surfeit**	surplus
flout	mock	**heresy**	false religious belief
good sooth	in truth, indeed	**swoon**	faint
perforce	of necessity	**nigh**	near

HELENA Wherefore was I to this keen mockery born?
        When at your hands did I deserve this scorn?   130
        Is't not enough, is't not enough, young man,
        That I did never, no, nor never can
        Deserve a sweet look from Demetrius' eye
        But you must flout my insufficiency?
        Good troth, you do me wrong, good sooth, you do,   135
        In such disdainful manner me to woo!
        But fare you well: perforce I must confess
        I thought you lord of more true gentleness.
        O, that a lady of one man refused
        Should of another therefore be abused!   *Exit*   140
LYSANDER She sees not Hermia. Hermia, sleep thou there,
        And never mayst thou come Lysander near.
        For, as a surfeit of the sweetest things
        The deepest loathing to the stomach brings,
        Or as the heresies that men do leave   145
        Are hated most of those they did deceive,
        So thou, my surfeit and my heresy,
        Of all be hated, but the most of me!
        And, all my powers, address your love and might
        To honour Helen, and to be her knight.   *Exit*   150
HERMIA [*Waking*.]
        Help me, Lysander, help me! Do thy best
        To pluck this crawling serpent from my breast!
        Ay me, for pity! What a dream was here!
        Lysander, look how I do quake with fear –
        Methought a serpent ate my heart away,   155
        And you sat smiling at his cruel prey.
        Lysander! What, removed? Lysander, lord!
        What, out of hearing? Gone? No sound, no word?
        Alack, where are you? Speak and if you hear.
        Speak, of all loves! I swoon almost with fear.   160
        No? Then I well perceive you are not nigh.
        Either death or you I'll find immediately.   *Exit*

53

Looking back at Act 2

Activities for groups or individuals

What impression of the fairy world do you get from this photograph?
What do you think Oberon should look like on stage?

1 Love is the drug

The fairies' perception of the world is different from that of the mortals. It could be presented as a drug-induced state with the fairies intoxicated or 'high'. The flower could also act as a kind of hallucinogen which changes people's perceptions of others. Does this interpretation work?

2 Love as magic

In Scene 1, lines 155–74, Oberon tells of the flower whose juice on a sleeper's eyelids makes them 'madly dote' on the first person they see when they wake. The idea of love potions is ancient, but even today the connection is often made between love and magic. Discuss why this might be.

3 Who's who?

Many people get confused between the lovers in *A Midsummer Night's Dream*, particularly when the lovers begin to swap and change who loves who.

Experiment with ways to remember which lover is which in terms of their distinct characteristics.

For example:

Helena is tall
Hermia is small

Helena might be dressed in yellow
Hermia might be dressed in brown

Carry on playing with similar ideas. How might a director help the audience separate Lysander and Demetrius?

4 Oberon – the master?

In his two speeches on page 43, Oberon shows his power over the lives of both mortals and fairies. There is a sense in which the male characters dominate the play (for example, Theseus in Athens, Oberon in the wood). Perhaps this is simply Shakespeare reflecting the prejudices (and realities?) of his time. Or perhaps it is the fact that they have positions of great power (duke, king). Discuss whether this male domination makes any difference to your responses to the characters or to the play.

5 Update lines 81–117 in Scene 1

You are involved in co-scripting a modern version of *A Midsummer Night's Dream*. Your director wants to keep the original 'forgeries of jealousy' speech, but you want to update it to make it appeal to a very wide audience. Come up with some suggestions for the script-writing team as to how this could be done.

In the wood near the sleeping Titania, the Mechanicals begin their rehearsal with Bottom suggesting changes in the play to make it less frightening.

Create a caption for this photograph of the Mechanicals.

Pat on the dot, on time
brake thicket
tiring-house dressing room
bully adjective that implies respect
and admiration

By'r lakin by our lady
(an exclamation)
parlous perilous

ACT 3   SCENE 1
The wood

Enter the Clowns [, BOTTOM, QUINCE, SNOUT, STARVELING, SNUG
and FLUTE. TITANIA remains on stage, asleep]

BOTTOM Are we all met?

QUINCE Pat, pat; and here's a marvellous convenient place for our
rehearsal. This green plot shall be our stage, this hawthorn brake
our tiring-house, and we will do it in action as we will do it before
the Duke. 5

BOTTOM Peter Quince!

QUINCE What sayest thou, bully Bottom?

BOTTOM There are things in this comedy of Pyramus and Thisbe that
will never please. First, Pyramus must draw a sword to kill himself,
which the ladies cannot abide. How answer you that? 10

SNOUT By'r lakin, a parlous fear!

STARVELING I believe we must leave the killing out, when all is done.

BOTTOM Not a whit; I have a device to make all well. Write me a
prologue, and let the prologue seem to say we will do no harm with
our swords, and that Pyramus is not killed indeed; and for the more 15
better assurance, tell them that I, Pyramus, am not Pyramus, but
Bottom the weaver: this will put them out of fear.

QUINCE Well, we will have such a prologue; and it shall be written in
eight and six.

BOTTOM No, make it two more: let it be written in eight and eight. 20

SNOUT Will not the ladies be afeard of the lion?

STARVELING I fear it, I promise you.

BOTTOM Masters, you ought to consider with yourself, to bring in (God
shield us!) a lion among ladies is a most dreadful thing; for there
is not a more fearful wildfowl than your lion living; and we ought 25
to look to't.

SNOUT Therefore another prologue must tell he is not a lion.

BOTTOM Nay, you must name his name, and half his face must be seen
through the lion's neck, and he himself must speak through, saying
thus, or to the same defect: 'Ladies', or 'Fair ladies, I would wish 30
you', or 'I would request you', or 'I would entreat you, not to fear,
not to tremble: my life for yours. If you think I come hither as
a lion, it were pity of my life. No, I am no such thing; I am a man,

*The Mechanicals discuss how to show moonlight and
the wall in the play, and decide they must have
an actor represent each.*

1 Bottom's play (in groups of six)

Of course it is Quince's play, but Bottom certainly has ideas for it.
Look at Bottom's suggestions on pages 57 and 59, reading them
aloud, and then talking about them (and what they tell you about
Bottom himself). Improvise the additions and changes suggested
here (with Quince doing the Prologue, Snug playing the lion,
Starveling the moon and Snout the wall).

2 What do they think of Bottom? (in groups of six)

Each person take on the role of one of the Mechanicals. Explain
what your character thinks of Bottom from what he says and does
in lines 1–59. Include what Bottom thinks of himself. Then talk
about what you personally think about Bottom and compare it with
the Mechanicals' view.

3 A rehearsal within a play? (in pairs)

Not only is there a play within *A Midsummer Night's Dream*, there
are even rehearsals. Perhaps Shakespeare was mocking amateur
dramatics because he was in one of the very first professional
theatre companies in England. What other reasons might there be?

4 Watch your language (in pairs)

The Mechanicals don't just speak in prose, they use a less formal,
less literary kind of language. Write a short scene of modern
workers rehearsing (feel free to exaggerate). Write another short
scene with middle-class, or literary and artistic people (again, exaggerate if you want). Compare the kind of language each group uses.

---

casement hinged window
loam clay for brick making

rough-cast rough coating for a
wall

as other men are' – and there indeed let him name his name, and
tell them plainly he is Snug the joiner.   35

QUINCE Well, it shall be so. But there is two hard things: that is, to
bring the moonlight into a chamber; for, you know, Pyramus and
Thisbe meet by moonlight.

SNUG Doth the moon shine that night we play our play?

BOTTOM A calendar, a calendar! Look in the almanac – find out   40
moonshine, find out moonshine!

QUINCE Yes, it doth shine that night.

BOTTOM Why, then may you leave a casement of the great chamber
window, where we play, open, and the moon may shine in at the
casement.   45

QUINCE Ay; or else one must come in with a bush of thorns and a
lantern, and say he comes to disfigure, or to present the person of
Moonshine. Then there is another thing: we must have a wall in
the great chamber; for Pyramus and Thisbe, says the story, did talk
through the chink of a wall.   50

SNOUT You can never bring in a wall. What say you, Bottom?

BOTTOM Some man or other must present Wall; and let him have some
plaster, or some loam, or some rough-cast about him to signify Wall;
or let him hold his fingers thus, and through that cranny shall
Pyramus and Thisbe whisper.   55

QUINCE If that may be, then all is well. Come, sit down every mother's
son, and rehearse your parts. Pyramus, you begin. When you have
spoken your speech, enter into that brake, and so everyone
according to his cue.

Puck enters, and watches as the Mechanicals begin to rehearse, going off with Bottom when he goes off stage. After getting his lines muddled, Flute gives Bottom his cue to reappear.

1 How to be invisible

Puck is invisible here (in that the Mechanicals can't see him although the audience can). Think how you might act this as the Mechanicals continue their rehearsal.

2 Acting badly is good (in pairs)

Talk about the complications of acting characters who are attempting to act well, but failing. Suggest how the timing of the lines opposite might help to bring out the Mechanicals' bad acting.

3 The transformation (I) (in groups of six to seven)

Rehearse and act out lines 60–106. The farce of the rehearsal turns into the farce of Bottom being an ass, but it offers lots of opportunity for knockabout comedy. If you can, video the scene, using close-ups and cuts, or perform it directly to the rest of the class.

4 The transformation (II)

There are many myths about people being transformed into animals, including asses. Bottom is something of an ass (fool) already. Some people have seen a darker side to his transformation to a real ass, associating the ass with sexual prowess. Others see it as a mockery of romance. Thinking about this, look at the photographs on pages 62, 64 and 66 – which do you prefer?

---

hempen homespuns the Mechanicals are dressed in rough, homemade clothes

lily white of hue pale coloured
brisky juvenal lively young man
eke also

Enter PUCK

PUCK What hempen homespuns have we swaggering here   60
      So near the cradle of the Fairy Queen?
      What, a play toward? I'll be an auditor,
      An actor too perhaps, if I see cause.
QUINCE Speak, Pyramus! Thisbe, stand forth!
BOTTOM (*as Pyramus*)
      Thisbe, the flowers of odious savours sweet –   65
QUINCE Odours – 'odorous'!
BOTTOM (*as Pyramus*)   ...odours savours sweet.
     So hath thy breath, my dearest Thisbe dear.
     But hark, a voice! Stay thou but here awhile,
     And by and by I will to thee appear.   *Exit* 70
PUCK A stranger Pyramus than e'er played here.   [*Exit*]
FLUTE Must I speak now?
QUINCE Ay, marry must you; for you must understand he goes but to
    see a noise that he heard, and is to come again.
FLUTE (*as Thisbe*)
     Most radiant Pyramus, most lilywhite of hue,   75
      Of colour like the red rose on triumphant briar,
     Most brisky juvenal, and eke most lovely Jew,
      As true as truest horse that yet would never tire,
     I'll meet thee, Pyramus, at Ninny's tomb –
QUINCE 'Ninus' tomb', man! – Why, you must not speak that yet; that   80
    you answer to Pyramus. You speak all your part at once, cues and
    all. Pyramus, enter – your cue is past. It is 'never tire'.
FLUTE O –
    (*as Thisbe*)
    As true as truest horse, that yet would never tire.

Bottom re-enters with an ass' head (because of Puck's magic), and all his comrades run away. Bottom thinks that they are teasing him to make him frightened.

'O Bottom, thou art changed. What do I see on thee?' In the Royal National Theatre's 1992 production of *A Midsummer Night's Dream*, Puck's feet became Bottom's ass' ears.

knavery trick/s
ousel blackbird
cock male bird

throstle song thrush
little quill quiet song

Enter PUCK, *and* BOTTOM *with the ass head on*

BOTTOM (*as Pyramus*)
  If I were fair, fair Thisbe, I were only thine.   85
QUINCE O monstrous! O strange! We are haunted! Pray, masters, fly,
 masters! Help!
       Exeunt Quince, Snug, Flute, Snout and Starveling
PUCK I'll follow you: I'll lead you about a round,
  Through bog, through bush, through brake, through briar;
  Sometime a horse I'll be, sometime a hound,   90
   A hog, a headless bear, sometime a fire,
  And neigh, and bark, and grunt, and roar, and burn,
  Like horse, hound, hog, bear, fire at every turn. *Exit*
BOTTOM Why do they run away? This is a knavery of them to make
 me afeard.   95

Enter SNOUT

SNOUT O Bottom, thou art changed. What do I see on thee?
BOTTOM What do you see? You see an ass head of your own, do you?
          [*Exit Snout*]

Enter QUINCE

QUINCE Bless thee, Bottom, bless thee! Thou art translated! *Exit*
BOTTOM I see their knavery. This is to make an ass of me, to fright
 me, if they could; but I will not stir from this place, do what they 100
 can. I will walk up and down here, and will sing, that they shall
 hear I am not afraid.
 [*Sings.*] The ousel cock so black of hue,
   With orange-tawny bill,
   The throstle with his note so true,   105
   The wren with little quill –

Bottom's song wakes Titania who instantly falls in love with him, and vows to keep him with her.

1 Transformations (in pairs)

Think about the transformations in lines 107–36. Bottom's behaviour and speech might change (as his head has done) to become more like a real ass. The transformed Titania is behaving differently from when she confronted Oberon. Experiment with tone, movement and manner for both characters and act out the lines.

2 'Reason and love keep little company ...' (in pairs)

What has been the relationship between reason and love in the play so far? Identify those characters who are being reasonable, and those who are dominated by their emotions, particularly love.

'What angel wakes me from my flowery bed?' Line 107 is one of Shakespeare's most famous lines, even though it is ironic. Why?

---

set his wit to
  set his wits against, argue with
give ... the lie
  contradict, call a liar
enthrallèd captivated

gleek joke
still doth tend always attends
purge ... grossness
  remove human coarseness

TITANIA [*Waking.*] What angel wakes me from my flowery bed?

BOTTOM [*Sings.*]

> The finch, the sparrow, and the lark,
> > The plainsong cuckoo grey,
> Whose note full many a man doth mark   110
> > And dares not answer nay –

for indeed, who would set his wit to so foolish a bird? Who would
give a bird the lie, though he cry 'cuckoo' never so?

TITANIA I pray thee, gentle mortal, sing again;
> Mine ear is much enamoured of thy note.   115
> So is mine eye enthrallèd to thy shape,
> And thy fair virtue's force perforce doth move me
> On the first view to say, to swear, I love thee.

BOTTOM Methinks, mistress, you should have little reason for that. And
yet, to say the truth, reason and love keep little company together   120
nowadays; the more the pity that some honest neighbours will not
make them friends. Nay, I can gleek upon occasion.

TITANIA Thou art as wise as thou art beautiful.

BOTTOM Not so neither; but if I had wit enough to get out of this wood,
I have enough to serve mine own turn.   125

TITANIA Out of this wood do not desire to go:
> Thou shalt remain here, whether thou wilt or no.
> I am a spirit of no common rate;
> The summer still doth tend upon my state,
> And I do love thee. Therefore go with me.   130
> I'll give thee fairies to attend on thee,
> And they shall fetch thee jewels from the deep,
> And sing, while thou on pressèd flowers dost sleep;
> And I will purge thy mortal grossness so
> That thou shalt like an airy spirit go.   135
> Peaseblossom, Cobweb, Moth, and Mustardseed!

Enter four Fairies.

PEASEBLOSSOM Ready.

COBWEB And I.

MOTH And I.

MUSTARDSEED And I.   140

Titania asks her fairies to look after Bottom.
He learns their names. Bottom is then led to Titania's bower.

Bottom, lifted by the fairies. This is the only meeting of the fairy and mortal worlds in the play, in that Bottom can see and talk to the fairies. Bottom and Titania have been transformed (in a sense they are having visions or dreams). Discuss what sort of relationship the two have. Use the photograph above as part of your discussions.

dewberries blackberries	**If I cut my finger ...** cobwebs
cry ... mercy beg your pardon	were used to stop bleeding

ALL Where shall we go?

TITANIA Be kind and courteous to this gentleman:
Hop in his walks and gambol in his eyes;
Feed him with apricocks and dewberries,
With purple grapes, green figs, and mulberries;   145
The honey-bags steal from the humble-bees,
And for night-tapers crop their waxen thighs,
And light them at the fiery glow-worms' eyes
To have my love to bed, and to arise;
And pluck the wings from painted butterflies   150
To fan the moonbeams from his sleeping eyes.
Nod to him, elves, and do him courtesies.

PEASEBLOSSOM Hail, mortal!

COBWEB Hail!

MOTH Hail!   155

MUSTARDSEED Hail!

BOTTOM I cry your worships mercy, heartily. I beseech your worship's
name.

COBWEB Cobweb.

BOTTOM I shall desire you of more acquaintance, good Master Cobweb;   160
if I cut my finger I shall make bold with you. Your name, honest
gentleman?

PEASEBLOSSOM Peaseblossom.

BOTTOM I pray you commend me to Mistress Squash, your mother,
and to Master Peascod, your father. Good Master Peaseblossom,   165
I shall desire you of more acquaintance, too. – Your name, I
beseech you, sir?

MUSTARDSEED Mustardseed.

BOTTOM Good Master Mustardseed, I know your patience well. That
same cowardly, giant-like ox-beef hath devoured many a gentleman   170
of your house. I promise you, your kindred hath made my eyes
water ere now. I desire you of more acquaintance, good Master
Mustardseed.

TITANIA Come, wait upon him. Lead him to my bower.
The moon methinks looks with a watery eye,   175
And when she weeps, weeps every little flower,
Lamenting some enforcèd chastity.
Tie up my lover's tongue; bring him silently.

Exeunt

Oberon wonders who or what Titania now loves.
Puck says she loves a 'monster' and explains what he has done to
Bottom and the other Mechanicals.

---

1 Puck's view of the Mechanicals
(in groups of four to six)

One person speaks Puck's lines 6–34, with the others miming the
Mechanicals' behaviour, and then talk about his view of them (for
example, he calls Bottom 'The shallowest thick-skin of that barren
sort').

2 See it – or hear it? (in groups of four to six)

Remind yourselves of what happened earlier in Scene 1, lines
85–107, and compare it with Puck's description opposite. Then
consider which you find most effective. Suggest why Shakespeare
relates as a story what the audience has just seen on stage.

3 Invent some comparisons (in pairs)

Lines 20–3 are an extended comparison of the Mechanicals and the
birds scattering. Compose some extended comparisons yourself,
trying to invent ones that capture the Mechanicals' confusion.
Write first in prose, and then in couplets. Read them aloud and
discuss which was easier to write.

---

close secret
consecrated sacred
patches clowns
rude rough
nole head
mimic actor

fowler bird-hunter
russet-pated choughs
 grey-headed jackdaws
apparel clothes
yielders
 those running away in fear

ACT 3 SCENE 2
The wood

Enter OBERON, *King of Fairies*

OBERON I wonder if Titania be awaked;
      Then what it was that next came in her eye,
      Which she must dote on, in extremity.

Enter PUCK

      Here comes my messenger. How now, mad spirit?
      What night-rule now about this haunted grove?   5
PUCK My mistress with a monster is in love.
      Near to her close and consecrated bower,
      While she was in her dull and sleeping hour,
      A crew of patches, rude mechanicals,
      That work for bread upon Athenian stalls,   10
      Were met together to rehearse a play
      Intended for great Theseus' nuptial day.
      The shallowest thick-skin of that barren sort,
      Who Pyramus presented, in their sport
      Forsook his scene and entered in a brake,   15
      When I did him at this advantage take:
      An ass's nole I fixèd on his head.
      Anon his Thisbe must be answerèd,
      And forth my mimic comes. When they him spy –
      As wild geese that the creeping fowler eye,   20
      Or russet-pated choughs, many in sort,
      Rising and cawing at the gun's report,
      Sever themselves and madly sweep the sky –
      So at his sight away his fellows fly,
      And at our stamp here o'er and o'er one falls;   25
      He 'Murder!' cries, and help from Athens calls.
      Their sense thus weak, lost with their fears thus strong,
      Made senseless things begin to do them wrong,
      For briars and thorns at their apparel snatch,
      Some sleeves, some hats; from yielders all things catch.   30

Oberon is pleased to hear that Titania has fallen in love with Bottom. Puck says he has also dealt with the 'Athenian'. Demetrius tries to court Hermia who accuses him of having murdered Lysander.

1 Two worlds, two views (in groups of four)

Split into two pairs. One pair read and rehearse the Oberon/Puck conversation (lines 35–42 and lines 88–101), and the other the argument between Demetrius and Hermia (lines 43–81). Then read them one after the other. Afterwards, consider what difference it makes having these argument so close together and how the two worlds differ.

2 Darkness and confusion (in pairs)

Look at the argument between Hermia and Demetrius (lines 43–81), and find the words and images that best bring out the mood of these two. Then read aloud just those words and images. What effects do these images have on the mood of the play here?

3 An unusual image (in pairs)

Hermia's image in lines 53–5 of the earth having a hole bored in it large enough for the moon to pass through and then annoy the sun (the moon's 'brother') with 'th'Antipodes' (those who live on the opposite side of the earth), is unusual to say the least. It is something like some of Titania's speech in Act 2 Scene 1, lines 81–117 in that it suggests everything in the natural world is in disorder. Try writing your own image that expresses the impossible (although, of course, Lysander *did* steal away from Hermia). Do you think the language used by lovers is often full of exaggeration?

---

latched captured, mastered
chide talk angrily
dead pale as death

Venus in Roman mythology, the
  goddess of love
sphere orbit

I led them on in this distracted fear,
And left sweet Pyramus translated there;
When in that moment, so it came to pass,
Titania waked, and straightway loved an ass.
OBERON This falls out better than I could devise.   35
But hast thou yet latched the Athenian's eyes
With the love juice, as I did bid thee do?
PUCK I took him sleeping – that is finished too –
And the Athenian woman by his side,
That when he waked, of force she must be eyed.   40

Enter DEMETRIUS *and* HERMIA

OBERON Stand close: this is the same Athenian.
PUCK This is the woman, but not this the man.
DEMETRIUS O, why rebuke you him that loves you so?
Lay breath so bitter on your bitter foe.
HERMIA Now I but chide; but I should use thee worse,   45
For thou, I fear, hast given me cause to curse.
If thou hast slain Lysander in his sleep,
Being o'er shoes in blood, plunge in the deep,
And kill me too.
The sun was not so true unto the day   50
As he to me. Would he have stol'n away
From sleeping Hermia? I'll believe as soon
This whole earth may be bored, and that the moon
May through the centre creep, and so displease
Her brother's noontide with th'Antipodes.   55
It cannot be but thou hast murdered him:
So should a murderer look; so dead, so grim.
DEMETRIUS So should the murdered look, and so should I,
Pierced through the heart with your stern cruelty;
Yet you, the murderer, look as bright, as clear,   60
As yonder Venus in her glimmering sphere.
HERMIA What's this to my Lysander? Where is he?
Ah, good Demetrius, wilt thou give him me?
DEMETRIUS I had rather give his carcass to my hounds.

Hermia storms off, after accusing Demetrius of murder.
Demetrius, too tired to follow, goes to sleep. Oberon tells Puck to find
Helena in order to correct his mistake.

1 The lovers again (I) (in pairs)

Perhaps you have already discussed what the lovers were like in
Act 1 (see page 16). Look again at Hermia and Demetrius here.
Compare the two characters by speaking and listening to just his
speeches, and then just her speeches. Discuss the differences
between the two, perhaps comparing your impressions of them
here with those earlier in the play.

2 The lovers again (II) (in pairs)

Look again at lines 43–81. It isn't just different groups in the play,
such as the lovers and fairies, that have different views of the
world, but also different characters in those groups, such as Hermia
and Demetrius. Make notes on what Hermia thinks is going on
here, and what Demetrius thinks. Then relate it to how they are
behaving.

3 Oberon's intentions (in pairs)

Read the final exchange between Puck and Oberon (lines 94–101).
What does this tell you about Oberon and his motives in dealing
with the mortals?

4 Are men fickle? (in pairs)

Puck says 'one man holding troth,/A million fail' (for every man
who is true in love, a million are not). Debate whether men are
fickle in love, and whether they are more fickle than women.

---

cur coward	**fancy-sick** sick with love
worm snake	**cheer** face
heaviness weariness	**Tartar** central Asian warrior
misprision mistake	

HERMIA Out, dog! Out, cur! Thou driv'st me past the bounds   65
Of maiden's patience. Hast thou slain him then?
Henceforth be never numbered among men.
O, once tell true; tell true, even for my sake:
Durst thou have looked upon him being awake?
And hast thou killed him sleeping? O, brave touch!   70
Could not a worm, an adder do so much?
An adder did it; for with doubler tongue
Than thine, thou serpent, never adder stung.
DEMETRIUS You spend your passion on a misprised mood.
I am not guilty of Lysander's blood,   75
Nor is he dead, for aught that I can tell.
HERMIA I pray thee, tell me then that he is well.
DEMETRIUS And if I could, what should I get therefor?
HERMIA A privilege, never to see me more;
And from thy hated presence part I so.   80
See me no more, whether he be dead or no.   *Exit*
DEMETRIUS There is no following her in this fierce vein;
Here therefore for a while I will remain.
So sorrow's heaviness doth heavier grow
For debt that bankrupt sleep doth sorrow owe,   85
Which now in some slight measure it will pay,
If for his tender here I make some stay.
          [*He*] *lies down* [*and sleeps*].
OBERON What hast thou done? Thou hast mistaken quite,
And laid the love juice on some true love's sight.
Of thy misprision must perforce ensue   90
Some true love turned, and not a false turned true.
PUCK Then fate o'errules, that, one man holding troth,
A million fail, confounding oath on oath.
OBERON About the wood go swifter than the wind,
And Helena of Athens look thou find.   95
All fancy-sick she is and pale of cheer
With sighs of love, that costs the fresh blood dear.
By some illusion see thou bring her here;
I'll charm his eyes against she do appear.
PUCK I go, I go, look how I go!   100
Swifter than arrow from the Tartar's bow.   *Exit*

Oberon puts the magic juice on Demetrius' eyes, and Lysander enters with Helena. He is still trying to convince Helena that he loves her. She thinks he's lying.

1 Puck
(in groups of four to six)

List the ways in which Puck behaves and thinks like a child, on the evidence here and elsewhere. He seems pleased at the mayhem, and is rather insensitive to the motives and feelings of the lovers. Compare all this with the illustration.

Puck (from an eighteenth-century book).

2 Class direction (whole class)

The class will need two volunteers – one to play Puck and one to play Oberon. The class directs the actors through lines 88–121. Take all suggestions seriously, try them and evaluate them. Think about:

their relationship   movement   gestures   tone of voice
use of silence   everything that adds to dramatic effect

See if the class can come to a united decision about what works best in relation to their vision of the characters and the scene. To work, this needs creativity, confidence and, most importantly, respectful listening skills.

apple pupil	**befall prepost'rously**
fee reward	turn out absurdly and unnaturally
fond pageant foolish scene	**light as tales** fictional as stories

74

OBERON   [*Squeezing the juice on Demetrius' eyes.*]
            Flower of this purple dye,
            Hit with Cupid's archery,
            Sink in apple of his eye.
            When his love he doth espy,   105
            Let her shine as gloriously
            As the Venus of the sky.
            When thou wak'st, if she be by,
            Beg of her for remedy.

Enter PUCK

PUCK   Captain of our fairy band,   110
            Helena is here at hand,
            And the youth mistook by me,
            Pleading for a lover's fee.
            Shall we their fond pageant see?
            Lord, what fools these mortals be!   115
OBERON   Stand aside. The noise they make
            Will cause Demetrius to awake.
PUCK   Then will two at once woo one –
            That must needs be sport alone;
            And those things do best please me   120
            That befall prepost'rously.

Enter LYSANDER *and* HELENA

LYSANDER Why should you think that I should woo in scorn?
            Scorn and derision never come in tears.
          Look when I vow, I weep; and vows so born,
            In their nativity all truth appears.   125
          How can these things in me seem scorn to you,
          Bearing the badge of faith to prove them true?
HELENA You do advance your cunning more and more.
            When truth kills truth, O devilish-holy fray!
          These vows are Hermia's. Will you give her o'er?   130
            Weigh oath with oath, and you will nothing weigh;
          Your vows to her and me, put in two scales,
          Will even weigh, and both as light as tales.
LYSANDER I had no judgement when to her I swore.

Demetrius wakes, and tells Helena in very exaggerated language how much he loves her. She thinks that he is part of the plot to tease her.

1 The dance of the lovers – who loves whom? (III)

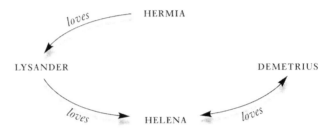

2 Colours

In the production shown here, the lovers wore white. A different production, shown on page 80, had the lovers in bright primary colours. What effect could the choice of costume colours have on the reading of both character and situation? Suggest some of your own ideas on how colour and lighting could be used in the lovers' scenes.

Taurus mountains in Turkey	**join in souls**	
courtesy courteous behaviour	work together wholeheartedly	
	trim neat, fine	

HELENA Nor none, in my mind, now you give her o'er.   135
LYSANDER Demetrius loves her, and he loves not you.
DEMETRIUS (*Waking.*)
        O Helen, goddess, nymph, perfect, divine!
        To what, my love, shall I compare thine eyne?
        Crystal is muddy! O, how ripe in show
        Thy lips, those kissing cherries, tempting grow!   140
        That pure congealèd white, high Taurus' snow,
        Fanned with the eastern wind, turns to a crow
        When thou hold'st up thy hand. O, let me kiss
        This princess of pure white, this seal of bliss!
HELENA O spite! O Hell! I see you all are bent   145
        To set against me for your merriment.
        If you were civil, and knew courtesy,
        You would not do me thus much injury.
        Can you not hate me, as I know you do,
        But you must join in souls to mock me too?   150
        If you were men, as men you are in show,
        You would not use a gentle lady so,
        To vow, and swear, and superpraise my parts,
        When I am sure you hate me with your hearts.
        You both are rivals, and love Hermia;   155
        And now both rivals to mock Helena.
        A trim exploit, a manly enterprise,
        To conjure tears up in a poor maid's eyes
        With your derision! None of noble sort
        Would so offend a virgin, and extort   160
        A poor soul's patience, all to make you sport.

Lysander and Demetrius argue over Helena. Hermia enters and asks Lysander why he left her. Lysander replies it is because he hates her.

---

1 The lovers at war (in groups of four)

'Lovers' hardly seems an apt description here. There seem to be two arguments: one between Lysander and Demetrius, and the other between Hermia and Lysander. Read through lines 162–91 a couple of times, developing the arguments as you see fit, and then adding in the movements and gestures. Who, if anyone, has your sympathy, or who do you laugh at?

2 Magic and being 'amazed' (in groups of five)

If you were directing the passage opposite you might choose to discriminate between the 'magic'd' men and the 'amazed' women who are not under the influence of the flower's magic. Try out ideas of how to do this with one person acting as director.

3 Onlookers (in groups of two to three)

Look at the photograph on page 80. When you read the play, it is easy to forget the presence of Puck and Oberon. But when you see it on stage their presence is always obvious. This kind of voyeurism – sitting in on the pain and confusion of others – surely does not reflect well on them. Would it be possible to present Puck and Oberon in a positive light here? How? Act out your ideas, concentrating on the involvement and responses of Puck and Oberon.

---

bequeath give
guest-wise sojourned
 stayed for a while, like a visitor
Disparage speak badly of
Lest unless

apprehension understanding
engilds the night
 gives the night a golden sheen
oes bright dress ornaments
 (or stars)

LYSANDER You are unkind, Demetrius: be not so,
        For you love Hermia – this you know I know –
        And here with all good will, with all my heart,
        In Hermia's love I yield you up my part;   165
        And yours of Helena to me bequeath,
        Whom I do love, and will do till my death.
HELENA Never did mockers waste more idle breath.
DEMETRIUS Lysander, keep thy Hermia; I will none.
        If e'er I loved her, all that love is gone.   170
        My heart to her but as guest-wise sojourned,
        And now to Helen is it home returned,
        There to remain.
LYSANDER   Helen, it is not so.
DEMETRIUS Disparage not the faith thou dost not know,
        Lest to thy peril thou aby it dear.   175
        Look where thy love comes: yonder is thy dear.

Enter HERMIA

HERMIA Dark night, that from the eye his function takes,
        The ear more quick of apprehension makes;
        Wherein it doth impair the seeing sense
        It pays the hearing double recompense.   180
        Thou art not by mine eye, Lysander, found;
        Mine ear, I thank it, brought me to thy sound.
        But why unkindly didst thou leave me so?
LYSANDER Why should he stay whom love doth press to go?
HERMIA What love could press Lysander from my side?   185
LYSANDER Lysander's love, that would not let him bide,
        Fair Helena – who more engilds the night
        Than all yon fiery oes and eyes of light.
        [*To Hermia*] Why seek'st thou me? Could not this make
           thee know
        The hate I bare thee made me leave thee so?   190
HERMIA You speak not as you think; it cannot be.

Helena now thinks everyone is mocking her, and complains that Hermia should behave better as they have been such close friends for so long.

The lovers watched intently by Puck. Which line do you think is being spoken?

confederacy plot
Injurious wrongful, harmful
bait torment

chid scolded
sampler piece of embroidery
incorporate united in one body

HELENA Lo, she is one of this confederacy!
        Now I perceive they have conjoined all three
        To fashion this false sport in spite of me.
        Injurious Hermia, most ungrateful maid,   195
        Have you conspired, have you with these contrived
        To bait me with this foul derision?
        Is all the counsel that we two have shared,
        The sisters' vows, the hours that we have spent
        When we have chid the hasty-footed time   200
        For parting us – O, is all forgot?
        All schooldays' friendship, childhood innocence?
        We, Hermia, like two artificial gods
        Have with our needles created both one flower,
        Both on one sampler, sitting on one cushion,   205
        Both warbling of one song, both in one key,
        As if our hands, our sides, voices, and minds
        Had been incorporate. So we grew together
        Like to a double cherry, seeming parted,
        But yet an union in partition,   210
        Two lovely berries moulded on one stem;
        So with two seeming bodies but one heart,
        Two of the first, like coats in heraldry,
        Due but to one, and crownèd with one crest.
        And will you rent our ancient love asunder,   215
        To join with men in scorning your poor friend?
        It is not friendly, 'tis not maidenly.
        Our sex, as well as I, may chide you for it,
        Though I alone do feel the injury.
HERMIA I am amazèd at your passionate words.   220
        I scorn you not; it seems that you scorn me.

Helena asks Hermia to have pity on her, and goes to leave because she's sure they are mocking her. Lysander offers to fight Demetrius for Helena.

---

1 The last relationship fails (in pairs)

Read through Helena's long speech (lines 192–219). Identify the images of positive relationships and childhood, and read them aloud with a partner. Think carefully about why they might be here.

2 Interviews (in groups of four)

Each take a part as one of the lovers. Write and rehearse a short monologue saying who you are, what had happened, how you feel and what you want to happen. Don't forget the constraints of the flower's magic, the strange night-time woodland world that the characters find themselves in, and their confused and emotional state. Video these monologues (if you can, otherwise just show them to the group). This idea can be developed by having interviews of each of the lovers where feelings and thoughts are explored. This too could be on video.

3 Acting? Things are not as they seem (in pairs)

Look carefully at lines 237–9. Why did Shakespeare choose to use such an image here, and how does it relate to the rest of the play?

4 Men fighting over women (in pairs)

Lines 249–56 seem rather stereotyped (and linked to the idea of male violence and male domination – why don't they just ask Helena?). But it seems to indicate that things are getting out of control. Predict some of the ways in which this conflict could end.

---

forsooth in truth
in grace in favour
Persever persevere, continue
counterfeit pretend

Make mouths pull faces
chronicled told (as a funny story)
argument
  subject (for making fun of)

HELENA Have you not set Lysander, as in scorn,
　　　　To follow me, and praise my eyes and face?
　　　　And made your other love, Demetrius,
　　　　Who even but now did spurn me with his foot,　　　225
　　　　To call me goddess, nymph, divine and rare,
　　　　Precious, celestial? Wherefore speaks he this
　　　　To her he hates? And wherefore doth Lysander
　　　　Deny your love, so rich within his soul,
　　　　And tender me, forsooth, affection,　　　　　　　230
　　　　But by your setting on, by your consent?
　　　　What though I be not so in grace as you,
　　　　So hung upon with love, so fortunate,
　　　　But miserable most, to love unloved:
　　　　This you should pity rather than despise.　　　　235
HERMIA I understand not what you mean by this.
HELENA Ay, do! Persever, counterfeit sad looks,
　　　　Make mouths upon me when I turn my back,
　　　　Wink each at other, hold the sweet jest up.
　　　　This sport, well carried, shall be chronicled.　　240
　　　　If you have any pity, grace, or manners,
　　　　You would not make me such an argument.
　　　　But fare ye well. 'Tis partly my own fault,
　　　　Which death or absence soon shall remedy.
LYSANDER Stay, gentle Helena: hear my excuse,　　　　245
　　　　My love, my life, my soul, fair Helena!
HELENA O, excellent!
HERMIA [*To Lysander*] Sweet, do not scorn her so.
DEMETRIUS If she cannot entreat, I can compel.
LYSANDER Thou canst compel no more than she entreat;
　　　　Thy threats have no more strength than her weak prayers.　250
　　　　Helen, I love thee, by my life, I do:
　　　　I swear by that which I will lose for thee
　　　　To prove him false that says I love thee not.
DEMETRIUS I say I love thee more than he can do.
LYSANDER If thou say so, withdraw, and prove it too.　　255
DEMETRIUS Quick, come.

Hermia clings on to Lysander as he insults her and tells her that he hates her and loves Helena.

---

1 Lysander's insults (in pairs)

Lysander's insults – 'Ethiop' and 'tawny Tartar' – sound extremely racist. The Elizabethans thought that a tan was unladylike and weather-beaten. Ladies didn't walk much in the open air – it was ordinary working people who had to be out in all weathers. If you were directing a production would you omit these insults? Make a case for your decision.

2 What an insult (I) (whole class)

As a class, make a list of all the insults in the play so far – there are quite a few. Number them and share them out, one each. Practise yours in a variety of ways and choose your favourite. Work around the class with everyone insulting everyone in turn. Repeat the activity adding appropriate gestures as you speak.

3 What an insult (II) (in small groups)

Choose four or five of your favourites from the class insult list. Use them as a basis for an improvisation. Show the class the results.

---

whereto tends all this
  what do you mean
tame   lacking in spirit
burr   prickly seed-case of a plant

bond   oath, legal agreement
weak bond   (Hermia's arms)
erewhile   recently

HERMIA   Lysander, whereto tends all this?

LYSANDER Away, you Ethiop!

DEMETRIUS   No, no, sir,
    Seem to break loose, take on as you would follow,
    But yet come not. You are a tame man, go.

LYSANDER Hang off, thou cat, thou burr! Vile thing, let loose,   260
    Or I will shake thee from me like a serpent.

HERMIA Why are you grown so rude? What change is this,
    Sweet love?

LYSANDER   Thy love? – out, tawny Tartar, out;
    Out, loathed medicine! O hated potion, hence!

HERMIA Do you not jest?

HELENA   Yes, sooth, and so do you.   265

LYSANDER Demetrius, I will keep my word with thee.

DEMETRIUS I would I had your bond, for I perceive
    A weak bond holds you. I'll not trust your word.

LYSANDER What? Should I hurt her, strike her, kill her dead?
    Although I hate her, I'll not harm her so.   270

HERMIA What? Can you do me greater harm than hate?
    Hate me? Wherefore? O me, what news, my love?
    Am not I Hermia? Are not you Lysander?
    I am as fair now as I was erewhile.
    Since night you loved me; yet since night you left me.   275
    Why then, you left me – O, the gods forbid! –
    In earnest, shall I say?

LYSANDER   Ay, by my life;
    And never did desire to see thee more.
    Therefore be out of hope, of question, of doubt;
    Be certain, nothing truer – 'tis no jest   280
    That I do hate thee and love Helena.

Hermia turns on Helena, and threatens to fight her,
thinking Helena has stolen Lysander's love.
Helena says she will return to Athens.

---

1 Hermia and Helena's insults (in pairs)

It seems as if Hermia is angered by Helena insulting her ('puppet') because she is short. She returns the insult, calling Helena 'thou painted maypole'. Discuss the attitudes current today about being short and being tall, and whether they are similar to the attitudes expressed by Helena and Hermia. Could an equivalent argument happen today?

2 'Let her not strike me' (in pairs)

The two women seem very close to physically fighting. Do your reactions to this differ from your reactions to the probability of the men fighting – and if so, why? In the play, is it purely for humour, or are there sinister undertones as well?

3 Love conceals, anger reveals (in small groups)

Read through the argument between Hermia and Helena in lines 282–344. Consider whether or not their characters are revealed more clearly here than in Act 1 (where some might say only their love was apparent). Is their relationship more complicated than this?

---

canker-blossom diseased flower
counterfeit cheat
prevailed with him
 won Lysander's love

curst fierce
shrewishness anger, scolding
chid scolded, rebuked

HERMIA [*To Helena*]
        O me, you juggler, you canker-blossom,
        You thief of love! What, have you come by night
        And stol'n my love's heart from him?

HELENA   Fine, i'faith!
        Have you no modesty, no maiden shame,   285
        No touch of bashfulness? What, will you tear
        Impatient answers from my gentle tongue?
        Fie, fie, you counterfeit, you puppet, you!

HERMIA 'Puppet'? Why so? – Ay, that way goes the game.
        Now I perceive that she hath made compare   290
        Between our statures; she hath urged her height,
        And with her personage, her tall personage,
        Her height, forsooth, she hath prevailed with him.
        And are you grown so high in his esteem
        Because I am so dwarfish and so low?   295
        How low am I, thou painted maypole? Speak!
        How low am I? I am not yet so low
        But that my nails can reach unto thine eyes.

HELENA I pray you, though you mock me, gentlemen,
        Let her not hurt me. I was never curst;   300
        I have no gift at all in shrewishness.
        I am a right maid for my cowardice;
        Let her not strike me. You perhaps may think
        Because she is something lower than myself
        That I can match her.

HERMIA   Lower? Hark, again!   305

HELENA Good Hermia, do not be so bitter with me.
        I evermore did love you, Hermia,
        Did ever keep your counsels, never wronged you,
        Save that in love unto Demetrius
        I told him of your stealth unto this wood.   310
        He followed you; for love I followed him,
        But he hath chid me hence, and threatened me
        To strike me, spurn me, nay, to kill me too.
        And now, so you will let me quiet go,
        To Athens will I bear my folly back,   315
        And follow you no further. Let me go;
        You see how simple and how fond I am.

Helena explains her fear of 'little' Hermia. Lysander and Demetrius leave to fight. Helena runs away, and Hermia follows.

1 Scuffle? (in groups of four)

Obviously, the men are keeping the women apart at one point at least (line 328). Find a space and, getting your clues from the speeches in lines 318–44, work out what each character is doing – who is standing where, to whom each speech is addressed, how to have the lovers go off stage, and so on. It's all very physical, and there are plenty of good insults. Then act it out. You may want to use the pictures on this page and on page 80 for inspiration.

minimus insignificant creature	**cheek by jowl** face to face
knot-grass a weed which was thought to stunt growth	**coil** turmoil
	'long because of
aby pay for	**fray** fight

HERMIA Why, get you gone! Who is't that hinders you?

HELENA A foolish heart that I leave here behind.

HERMIA What, with Lysander?

HELENA   With Demetrius.   320

LYSANDER Be not afraid; she shall not harm thee, Helena.

DEMETRIUS No, sir. She shall not, though you take her part.

HELENA O, when she is angry she is keen and shrewd;
          She was a vixen when she went to school,
          And though she be but little, she is fierce.   325

HERMIA Little again? Nothing but low and little?
          Why will you suffer her to flout me thus?
          Let me come to her.

LYSANDER   Get you gone, you dwarf,
          You minimus of hindering knot-grass made,
          You bead, you acorn.

DEMETRIUS   You are too officious   330
          In her behalf that scorns your services.
          Let her alone: speak not of Helena,
          Take not her part; for if thou dost intend
          Never so little show of love to her,
          Thou shalt aby it.

LYSANDER   Now she holds me not –   335
          Now follow, if thou dur'st, to try whose right,
          Of thine or mine, is most in Helena.

DEMETRIUS Follow? Nay, I'll go with thee, cheek by jowl.

                              Exeunt Lysander and Demetrius

HERMIA You, mistress, all this coil is 'long of you.
          Nay, go not back.

HELENA   I will not trust you, I,   340
          Nor longer stay in your curst company.
          Your hands than mine are quicker for a fray;
          My legs are longer, though, to run away!   *[Exit]*

HERMIA I am amazed, and know not what to say.   *Exit*

Puck explains his mistake. Oberon instructs him to lead Lysander and Demetrius astray by imitating their voices until all can be put right. In the meantime, he will 'beg' the Indian boy from Titania before releasing her from the charm.

1 It's not what you do, it's the way that you do it
(in pairs)

Lines 354–77 are another example in the play of a long speech that describes both speech and action. Explore some of the ways in which Puck and Oberon could play this scene, paying particular attention to what they do, and how they interact.

2 Puck and Oberon (in groups of three to four)

Lines 345–400 say a great deal about these two. Discuss whether you believe Puck (lines 347–51), what you think of Puck's love of sport and Oberon's hope for 'all things shall be peace'. Perhaps Oberon's speech (lines 388–95) says something about both of them. Consider the photograph on page 92, too – is Oberon manipulative but not malicious, or does he have Christ-like qualities of bringing love and harmony?

3 A promised restoration of order
(in groups of three to four)

Compare the language and imagery of lines 354–95 with the writing earlier in the scene, such as lines 257–305. The power of some of the images here seems to change how you are invited to look at events ('seem a dream and fruitless vision'). Think about the audience and discuss how they might react to the suggestion that everything that has happened might seem like just a dream.

---

sort turn out
welkin sky
Acheron one of the rivers in
 Hades, the underworld for the dead
testy bad tempered
bitter wrong sharp accusations

rail use abusive language
wonted usual
derision stupidity
league contract, agreement
date duration

Oberon and Puck come forward.

OBERON This is thy negligence. Still thou mistak'st,   345
        Or else committ'st thy knaveries wilfully.
PUCK Believe me, King of Shadows, I mistook.
        Did not you tell me I should know the man
        By the Athenian garments he had on?
        And so far blameless proves my enterprise   350
        That I have 'nointed an Athenian's eyes;
        And so far am I glad it so did sort,
        As this their jangling I esteem a sport.
OBERON Thou seest these lovers seek a place to fight:
        Hie therefore, Robin, overcast the night;   355
        The starry welkin cover thou anon
        With drooping fog as black as Acheron,
        And lead these testy rivals so astray
        As one come not within another's way.
        Like to Lysander sometime frame thy tongue,   360
        Then stir Demetrius up with bitter wrong,
        And sometime rail thou like Demetrius;
        And from each other look thou lead them thus,
        Till o'er their brows death-counterfeiting sleep
        With leaden legs and batty wings doth creep.   365
        Then crush this herb into Lysander's eye,
        Whose liquor hath this virtuous property,
        To take from thence all error with his might,
        And make his eyeballs roll with wonted sight.
        When they next wake, all this derision   370
        Shall seem a dream and fruitless vision,
        And back to Athens shall the lovers wend
        With league whose date till death shall never end.
        Whiles I in this affair do thee employ
        I'll to my Queen and beg her Indian boy;   375
        And then I will her charmèd eye release
        From monster's view, and all things shall be peace.

Day approaches, and though the fairies (unlike other spirits) can exist in the day, Oberon urges haste. Lysander returns and is misled by Puck.

Puck and Oberon. What line might be spoken here?

Aurora's harbinger signal of the
 dawn – the morning star
aye ever
consort keep company

Neptune god of the sea. The
 morning sun's beams turn the sea
 from green to 'yellow gold',
 transforming it
drawn with drawn sword
plainer more open

PUCK My fairy lord, this must be done with haste,
        For night's swift dragons cut the clouds full fast,
        And yonder shines Aurora's harbinger,   380
        At whose approach ghosts wandering here and there
        Troop home to churchyards. Damnèd spirits all,
        That in crossways and floods have burial,
        Already to their wormy beds are gone.
        For fear lest day should look their shames upon,   385
        They wilfully themselves exile from light,
        And must for aye consort with black-browed night.
OBERON But we are spirits of another sort.
        I with the morning's love have oft made sport,
        And like a forester the groves may tread   390
        Even till the eastern gate, all fiery-red,
        Opening on Neptune with fair blessèd beams,
        Turns into yellow gold his salt green streams.
        But notwithstanding, haste, make no delay;
        We may effect this business yet ere day.   [*Exit*] 395
PUCK   Up and down, up and down,
        I will lead them up and down;
        I am feared in field and town.
        Goblin, lead them up and down.
        Here comes one.   400

Enter LYSANDER

LYSANDER Where art thou, proud Demetrius? Speak thou now.
PUCK Here, villain, drawn and ready! Where art thou?
LYSANDER I will be with thee straight.
PUCK   Follow me then
        To plainer ground.

                    [*Exit Lysander*]

Puck misleads both Demetrius and Lysander by imitating their voices until they have both had enough and fall asleep.

---

1 Sleep sound (in groups of five)

Start by considering how Puck should imitate Lysander's voice well enough to fool Demetrius (and, a little later, imitate Demetrius' own voice). Then read through lines 401–63, working out how to get all the lovers asleep near one another. The stage direction just reads *Sleeps*, but in many productions, Puck takes a very direct part in getting the men to sleep.

2 To sleep, perchance to dream

Although there has been a night and dreams, at the end of the scene the lovers are asleep. Write down the thoughts and feelings of each as they drift into sleep, or write about his/her dreams.

3 Men versus women (in pairs)

Compare the speeches of the male lovers with those of the female lovers (lines 401–63). One person read the male speeches, the other the female. Consider what Puck says here as well (see Activity 2 on page 96). Join with another group and share your findings.

---

recreant   coward, villain
defiled   made dirty
lighter-heeled   faster
Abide   face

wot   know
buy this dear   suffer, pay dearly
To measure out my length
   to lie down

Enter DEMETRIUS

DEMETRIUS   Lysander, speak again.
    Thou runaway, thou coward, art thou fled?   405
    Speak! In some bush? Where dost thou hide thy head?
PUCK Thou coward, art thou bragging to the stars,
    Telling the bushes that thou look'st for wars,
    And wilt not come? Come, recreant, come, thou child,
    I'll whip thee with a rod. He is defiled   410
    That draws a sword on thee.
DEMETRIUS   Yea, art thou there?
PUCK Follow my voice. We'll try no manhood here.

                                    Exeunt

Enter LYSANDER

LYSANDER He goes before me, and still dares me on;
    When I come where he calls, then he is gone.
    The villain is much lighter-heeled than I;   415
    I followed fast, but faster he did fly,
    That fallen am I in dark uneven way,
    And here will rest me. (*Lies down.*) Come, thou gentle day,
    For if but once thou show me thy grey light
    I'll find Demetrius and revenge this spite. [*Sleeps.*]   420

Enter PUCK *and* DEMETRIUS

PUCK Ho, ho, ho! Coward, why com'st thou not?
DEMETRIUS Abide me if thou dar'st, for well I wot
    Thou runn'st before me, shifting every place,
    And dar'st not stand nor look me in the face.
    Where art thou now?
PUCK   Come hither; I am here.   425
DEMETRIUS Nay then, thou mock'st me. Thou shalt buy this dear
    If ever I thy face by daylight see.
    Now, go thy way; faintness constraineth me
    To measure out my length on this cold bed.
    By day's approach look to be visited. [*Sleeps.*]   430

Helena and Hermia enter separately, exhausted, and fall asleep. Puck puts the magic juice on Lysander's eyes to make him love Hermia again.

1 He's behind you! (in groups of five)

Present the end of this scene – which has a slapstick feel to it – like a pantomime. Try to include as many pantomime clichés as you can. Start from line 396.

2 Puck – a knavish lad (in pairs)

Look closely at what Puck says about women in lines 139–41 and lines 453–63. What kind of attitude does he appear to have towards them?

3 The lovers come together in peace? (in pairs)

Somehow, after the conflicts of Acts 1, 2 and 3, the lovers are now united (if only physically here – lying asleep beside each other). On a literal level, this is because of the fairies. What might this union, this being together, be on other levels? You can find some ideas about this on page 154.

4 The awakening (in groups of four)

Improvise a scene immediately following this where the lovers wake up and discover that they are now neatly sorted out into couples. How confused or amazed are they? What do they remember? How do they decipher the dream from reality? How have the experiences affected the relationships?

Abate diminish, cut short
curst bad-tempered
Bedabbled stained

Jack shall have Jill ... the man shall have his mare again
proverbs of Shakespeare's time for 'boy gets girl'

Enter HELENA

HELENA O weary night, O long and tedious night,
    Abate thy hours, shine comforts from the east,
That I may back to Athens by daylight
    From these that my poor company detest;
And sleep, that sometimes shuts up sorrow's eye,   435
Steal me awhile from mine own company. (*Sleeps.*)
PUCK   Yet but three? Come one more,
    Two of both kinds makes up four.
    Here she comes, curst and sad.
    Cupid is a knavish lad   440
    Thus to make poor females mad.

Enter HERMIA

HERMIA Never so weary, never so in woe,
    Bedabbled with the dew, and torn with briars –
I can no further crawl, no further go;
    My legs can keep no pace with my desires.   445
Here will I rest me till the break of day.
Heavens shield Lysander, if they mean a fray. [*Sleeps.*]
PUCK   On the ground
    Sleep sound.
    I'll apply   450
    To your eye,
    Gentle lover, remedy.
    [*Squeezes the juice on Lysander's eyes.*]
    When thou wak'st,
    Thou tak'st
    True delight   455
    In the sight
    Of thy former lady's eye;
    And the country proverb known,
    That every man should take his own,
    In your waking shall be shown.   460
    Jack shall have Jill,
    Naught shall go ill:
The man shall have his mare again, and all shall be well.
    [*Exit Puck;*] *the lovers remain on stage, asleep*

Looking back at Act 3

Activities for groups or individuals

1 Midsummer dream – or nightmare?

There are many nightmarish things about this play – for example, being turned into an ass, or Hermia's nightmare of the snake. Describe, paint or draw a memorable dream you have had. Then, in groups, relate your dreams and nightmares, and see if you can analyse each other's. Discuss whether you believe dreams have any significance.

The Scream by Edvard Munch.

2 What's Bottom like? Brainstorm!

Write the words 'Nick Bottom the weaver' in the centre of a large sheet of paper. Write around his name everything that comes to mind about the character. Spend about ten minutes on this brainstorming activity, then compare what you have done with other students' views.

3 Who knows Bottom?

We sometimes listen to what other people say about our friends. What do other Mechanicals think about Bottom? Consider each one in turn and say what you imagine is their perception of Bottom. Who knows him best?

4 Two characters – and three worlds

Bottom and Puck will take part in all three worlds (Mechanicals, fairies and court). What have they got in common, and what would they say to each other if they had a conversation? Improvise a meeting between the two characters in which they talk together about how alike and unalike they are.

5 The world in the woods

Use some of the following to help you visualise the play.

a *A map*: devise a map of Athens and the wood. The play gives some distances, but think about Titania's bower in relation to the space found by the Mechanicals for rehearsals. Also locate the situations for the various lovers' scenes.

b *A display*: create a display that shows how you think the world of the woods should look on stage or film. You could use drawings, photographs, images, and so on.

c *A board game*: develop *A Midsummer Night's Dream* board game.

d *A stage set*: for professional stage productions, designers always make a detailed model set before proceeding to the full-sized version. Design your own stage set for the wood scenes.

e *A costume design*: design costumes for the fairy world. There is much imagery which connects the natural world and the woodland, in particular with the fairies. How would you work in this connection through costume and colour? As you design costumes for the fairy world, consider how you would dress the Mechanicals, the lovers and the court.

Bottom gives instructions to Titania's fairies,
to scratch him and find him food.

Bottom, Titania and the fairies. Identify the differences between the
picture above and the one on page 102. Begin with costume and
expression. Talk together about the mood or feeling that you think each
production created for the fairy world.

1 How has Bottom changed?

Use Bottom's speeches opposite to identify how he has changed.
Suggest how these changes might be put across on stage.

---

coy caress
neaf hand
Cavalery a gentleman
  (Bottom's mistake for 'cavalier')

tongs and the bones simple
  musical instruments
a peck of provender a little food
bottle bundle

ACT 4   SCENE 1
The wood

Enter TITANIA, Queen of Fairies, and BOTTOM, and fairies
[including PEASEBLOSSOM, COBWEB and MUSTARDSEED;] and the
King OBERON behind them

TITANIA Come, sit thee down upon this flowery bed
  While I thy amiable cheeks do coy,
  And stick musk-roses in thy sleek smooth head,
  And kiss thy fair large ears, my gentle joy.

BOTTOM Where's Peaseblossom?   5

PEASEBLOSSOM Ready.

BOTTOM Scratch my head, Peaseblossom. Where's Mounsieur
 Cobweb?

COBWEB Ready.

BOTTOM Mounsieur Cobweb, good Mounsieur, get you your weapons 10
 in your hand, and kill me a red-hipped humble-bee on the top of
 a thistle; and, good Mounsieur, bring me the honey-bag. Do not
 fret yourself too much in the action, Mounsieur; and, good
 Mounsieur, have a care the honey-bag break not; I would be loath
 to have you overflown with a honey-bag, signior. Where's Moun- 15
 sieur Mustardseed?

MUSTARDSEED Ready.

BOTTOM Give me your neaf, Mounsieur Mustardseed. Pray you, leave
 your courtesy, good Mounsieur.

MUSTARDSEED What's your will?   20

BOTTOM Nothing, good Mounsieur, but to help Cavalery Peaseblossom
 to scratch. I must to the barber's, Mounsieur, for methinks I am
 marvellous hairy about the face. And I am such a tender ass, if my
 hair do but tickle me, I must scratch.

TITANIA What, wilt thou hear some music, my sweet love? 25

BOTTOM I have a reasonable good ear in music. Let's have the tongs
 and the bones.

TITANIA Or say, sweet love, what thou desir'st to eat.

BOTTOM Truly, a peck of provender, I could munch your good dry oats.
 Methinks I have a great desire to a bottle of hay. Good hay, sweet 30
 hay hath no fellow.

Bottom and Titania sleep. Oberon talks to Puck about his pity for Titania, and how she has returned the changeling boy. He removes the spell on her.

Bottom says that he is sleepy. How does he react to Titania's lines 37–42? Does he look at her lovingly? Or does he appear complacent and self-satisfied? Does he ogle her? Is he already asleep? Make your suggestions.

1 'The fierce vexation of a dream' (in groups of four)

Discuss this description of the night's events from the lovers' point of view, and from the point of view of the other characters. Take each of the main words in lines 64–6 into account.

2 Seeing or imagining (in groups of four)

One person reads Oberon's speech while the rest mime the actions it describes. Then act out Oberon speaking to Puck only. Which do you feel is more effective: seeing or imagining?

exposition of another of Bottom's mistakes; surely he means disposition to?
woodbine bindweed
dotage foolishness
orient lustrous
swain lover

TITANIA I have a venturous fairy that shall seek
    The squirrel's hoard, and fetch thee new nuts.
BOTTOM I had rather have a handful or two of dried peas. But, I pray
  you, let none of your people stir me; I have an exposition of sleep 35
  come upon me.
TITANIA Sleep thou, and I will wind thee in my arms.
    Fairies be gone, and be all ways away. [*Exeunt Fairies*]
    So doth the woodbine the sweet honeysuckle
    Gently entwist; the female ivy so 40
    Enrings the barky fingers of the elm.
    O, how I love thee! How I dote on thee!
      [*They sleep.*]

    Enter PUCK. OBERON *comes forward*

OBERON Welcome, good Robin. Seest thou this sweet sight?
    Her dotage now I do begin to pity;
    For, meeting her of late behind the wood 45
    Seeking sweet favours for this hateful fool,
    I did upbraid her and fall out with her,
    For she his hairy temples then had rounded
    With coronet of fresh and fragrant flowers;
    And that same dew, which sometime on the buds 50
    Was wont to swell like round and orient pearls,
    Stood now within the pretty flowerets' eyes
    Like tears that did their own disgrace bewail.
    When I had at my pleasure taunted her,
    And she in mild terms begged my patience, 55
    I then did ask of her her changeling child,
    Which straight she gave me, and her fairy sent
    To bear him to my bower in Fairyland.
    And now I have the boy, I will undo
    This hateful imperfection of her eyes. 60
    And, gentle Puck, take this transformèd scalp
    From off the head of this Athenian swain,
    That, he awaking when the other do,
    May all to Athens back again repair,
    And think no more of this night's accidents 65
    But as the fierce vexation of a dream.
    But first I will release the Fairy Queen.
      [*Squeezing a herb on Titania's eyes.*]

> *Titania wakes, and she and Oberon are reconciled.*
> *Puck removes the ass' head from Bottom. All leave except the*
> *'mortals' (the lovers and Bottom).*

---

1 'Methought I was enamoured of an ass' (in pairs)

One person act as Titania, waking from her vision, the other, Oberon. Improvise Titania's thoughts and feelings in a speech that tells Oberon about her 'vision', and then Oberon's comments and replies.

2 Music and dance (in pairs)

The resolution of the conflict between Titania and Oberon is marked by both dance and music. In Elizabethan times, the harmony of music was often taken as a symbol or sign of human harmony. What kind of music and dance would be suitable for this moment in the play? If you can, develop a short dance of Titania and Oberon, perhaps to some appropriate music you have found, or create your own.

3 The fairies, the lovers and Bottom (in small groups)

At this moment, all these characters are in the same place ('all these five' (line 79) are the lovers and Bottom on the ground). Discuss whether having all the characters together is significant, and why. The stage could look very littered. How would you position them all?

4 A change in Oberon's language?

Look carefully at the language Oberon uses in lines 82–89. How is it different from the language of his first speeches in Act 2, lines 60–80? Think of the possible reasons for this change.

---

wast wont   used, was accustomed
Dian's bud   the antidote to
  Cupid's flower?

amity   friendly relations
compass   go round

Be as thou wast wont to be;
See as thou wast wont to see.
Dian's bud o'er Cupid's flower   70
Hath such force and blessèd power.
Now, my Titania, wake you, my sweet Queen!

TITANIA *[Starting up.]*
My Oberon, what visions have I seen!
Methought I was enamoured of an ass.

OBERON There lies your love.

TITANIA   How came these things to pass?   75
O, how mine eyes do loathe his visage now!

OBERON Silence awhile: Robin, take off this head.
Titania, music call, and strike more dead
Than common sleep of all these five the sense.

TITANIA Music, ho, music such as charmeth sleep!   80
                    [Soft music plays.]

PUCK *[To Bottom, removing the ass's head]*
Now when thou wak'st, with thine own fool's eyes peep.

OBERON Sound, music! Come, my Queen, take hands with me,
And rock the ground whereon these sleepers be.
                    [They dance.]
Now thou and I are new in amity,
And will tomorrow midnight solemnly   85
Dance in Duke Theseus' house triumphantly,
And bless it to all fair prosperity.
There shall the pairs of faithful lovers be
Wedded, with Theseus, all in jollity.

PUCK   Fairy King, attend, and mark: 90
I do hear the morning lark.

OBERON   Then, my Queen, in silence sad,
Trip we after night's shade;
We the globe can compass soon,
Swifter than the wandering moon.   95

TITANIA   Come, my lord, and in our flight
Tell me how it came this night
That I sleeping here was found
With these mortals on the ground.
                    Exeunt Oberon, Titania and Puck

Theseus, Hippolyta and the others enter on an early morning hunting
expedition. After praising the baying of the hounds, they find the
sleeping lovers.

1 'Trip we after night's shade'

The transition between the entrance of the court and the exit of
the fairies at line 99 (page 105) is between the fairy world of
moonlight and the daylight world of Theseus. Decide how you
might signal this change on stage.

2 'The rite of May' (in groups of three to four)

Line 130 connects with the festivals of Tudor England (as does the
title of the play itself). In some of these festivals, ordinary
behaviour and laws were dispensed with. Festivals could include
disorder and people behaving free of ordinary constraints. In a way,
it was like the modern holiday when people do things they
wouldn't ordinarily do. Talk about how people can behave on
holiday, and compare that with how people behave in the play.

3 A word of warning?

Is the sudden remembrance of the threat (lines 132–4) to put
Hermia in a convent or execute her a real menacing moment? How
might Theseus speak these lines?

4 Can't Shakespeare count? (in pairs)

The play opens with 'Four nights will quickly dream away the
time', but now Hermia has to give her answer the next morning.
Seems a bit harsh: can't Shakespeare count? Suggest reasons why
Shakespeare might have done this. Also, how do they observe the
'rite of May' on a midsummer's night? Or doesn't it matter?

---

vaward early part
Uncouple unleash them
Cadmus
  mythical founder of Thebes

So flewed, so sanded
  with similar jowls and similar
  sandy colouring
dewlapped with loose neck skin
matched in mouth like bells
  loud like bells

Wind horns. Enter THESEUS *with* HIPPOLYTA, EGEUS, *and all his*
train.

THESEUS Go, one of you, find out the forester;   100
For now our observation is performed,
And since we have the vaward of the day,
My love shall hear the music of my hounds.
Uncouple in the western valley; let them go:
Dispatch, I say, and find the forester.   105
          [*Exit an Attendant*]
We will, fair Queen, up to the mountain's top,
And mark the musical confusion
Of hounds and echo in conjunction.
HIPPOLYTA I was with Hercules and Cadmus once,
When in a wood of Crete they bayed the bear   110
With hounds of Sparta: never did I hear
Such gallant chiding; for besides the groves,
The skies, the fountains, every region near
Seemed all one mutual cry. I never heard
So musical a discord, such sweet thunder.   115
THESEUS My hounds are bred out of the Spartan kind,
So flewed, so sanded; and their heads are hung
With ears that sweep away the morning dew;
Crook-kneed, and dewlapped like Thessalian bulls;
Slow in pursuit, but matched in mouth like bells,   120
Each under each. A cry more tuneable
Was never hallooed to nor cheered with horn
In Crete, in Sparta, nor in Thessaly.
Judge when you hear. But soft, what nymphs are these?
EGEUS My lord, this is my daughter here asleep,   125
And this Lysander; this Demetrius is,
This Helena, old Nedar's Helena.
I wonder of their being here together.
THESEUS No doubt they rose up early to observe
The rite of May, and hearing our intent   130
Came here in grace of our solemnity.
But speak, Egeus; is not this the day
That Hermia should give answer of her choice?
EGEUS It is, my lord.

The lovers are woken by shouts and blasts on horns. Lysander tries to explain what has happened, Egeus urges the duke to punish Lysander for attempting to elope with Hermia.

1 Three speeches, three views (in groups of three)

Each take a part, and read the opposite page aloud, thinking about the mood of each character. Together, talk about each speech, especially the images. Finally, present the state of mind of each character in a short monologue.

2 The dance of lovers – who loves whom? (IV)

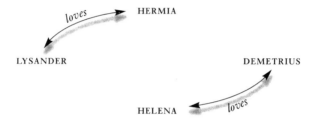

This is the final arrangement of the lovers. Look back at the 'dance' of the lovers on pages 10, 50 and 76. Putting all the dances together, identify what pattern emerges. Apply this method to the play, looking for patterns of day/night; Athens/wood; and others. Make charts/graphs/displays of your findings.

3 What do you think of Egeus?

A simple enough question – answer it, and present evidence to back up your conclusions.

4 Back to the beginning? (in groups of three)

Has the play now come full circle, with Egeus demanding his 'rights' and nothing changing, the whole 'dream' having had no effect on the real world, or ...? Discuss your responses.

Saint Valentine a popular belief was that birds chose their mates on Saint Valentine's Day

couple pair up
Without beyond
defeated cheated

THESEUS Go, bid the huntsmen wake them with their horns.   135
        Shout within; wind horns; [the lovers] all start up.
    Good morrow, friends. Saint Valentine is past;
    Begin these woodbirds but to couple now?
        [The lovers kneel.]
LYSANDER Pardon, my lord.
THESEUS   I pray you all, stand up.
    I know you two are rival enemies:
    How comes this gentle concord in the world,   140
    That hatred is so far from jealousy
    To sleep by hate, and fear no enmity?
LYSANDER My lord, I shall reply amazedly,
    Half sleep, half waking; but as yet, I swear,
    I cannot truly say how I came here.   145
    But as I think (for truly would I speak)
    And now I do bethink me, so it is –
    I came with Hermia hither. Our intent
    Was to be gone from Athens, where we might
    Without the peril of the Athenian law –   150
EGEUS Enough, enough, my lord; you have enough –
    I beg the law, the law upon his head!
    They would have stol'n away, they would, Demetrius,
    Thereby to have defeated you and me,
    You of your wife, and me of my consent,   155
    Of my consent that she should be your wife.

Demetrius explains his new-found love for Helena.
Theseus instructs the lovers to come with him to be married.
All leave except the lovers.

---

1 Demetrius – has he changed? (in pairs)

Compare Demetrius' speech opposite with one of his earlier
speeches. Pick one speech each, and read one, then the other,
trying to bring out Demetrius' mood and character. Go through
each speech, identifying the words and phrases that best capture
his personality (for example, 'I in fury'), and read just those parts
of speech. How has he changed – and why?

2 'Love' and 'dote' (in small groups)

Demetrius says his feelings for Hermia was mere 'doting', and his
feeling for Helena is now 'love'. Draw up a list of which
relationships in different parts of the play you think were 'doting'
and which 'love'. Then prepare a short presentation for the class
involving the whole group that gives your view of the difference
between the two feelings. Use this speech and others where you
can.

3 Theseus and Oberon (in groups of four to six)

At this moment Theseus is the dominant character (as he is in Act
I Scene I, lines 83–90, and other parts in the play). Read some of
his speeches aloud and then compare them with some of Oberon's.
Go on to talk about and list the similarities and differences between
the two characters. Do you feel that the fairy and mortal worlds
are dominated by men, or is it more complicated than that?

---

in fancy doting, in love
wot know
idle gaud worthless toy

overbear your will
overrule your wishes
something worn somewhat spent
(nearly over?)

DEMETRIUS My lord, fair Helen told me of their stealth,
Of this their purpose hither to this wood;
And I in fury hither followed them,
Fair Helena in fancy following me.   160
But, my good lord, I wot not by what power
(But by some power it is), my love to Hermia,
Melted as the snow, seems to me now
As the remembrance of an idle gaud
Which in my childhood I did dote upon;   165
And all the faith, the virtue of my heart,
The object and the pleasure of mine eye,
Is only Helena. To her, my lord,
Was I betrothed ere I saw Hermia;
But like a sickness did I loathe this food.   170
But, as in health come to my natural taste,
Now I do wish it, love it, long for it,
And will for evermore be true to it.
THESEUS Fair lovers, you are fortunately met.
Of this discourse we more will hear anon.   175
Egeus, I will overbear your will;
For in the temple, by and by, with us
These couples shall eternally be knit.
And, for the morning now is something worn,
Our purposed hunting shall be set aside.   180
Away with us to Athens. Three and three,
We'll hold a feast in great solemnity.
Come, Hippolyta.

Exit Theseus with Hippolyta, Egeus, and his train

The lovers wonder if they are dreaming, agree they are awake, and follow the duke. Bottom wakes, and wonders at his 'dream'.

---

1 Reading through (in groups of five)

Each take a part and read through the lines opposite. Then find a space and 'walk through' the lines as you read. Explore different ways of acting it out, especially movement and acting when *not* speaking.

2 It's not what you say, it's the way that you say it (in pairs)

Read the lovers' speeches (lines 184–96), and then Bottom's lines 197–211, and talk about the differences in the way they describe their experiences. You might like to compare Bottom's speech with I Corinthians 2.9. in the Bible:

> But as it is written, Eye hath not seen, nor ear heard, neither have entered into the heart of man, the things which God hath prepared for them that love him.

There are also parallels with Titania's dazed state (in Act 4 Scene 1, lines 73–99). The different worlds of the fairies, the lovers and the Mechanicals all meet at this point – or do they?

3 Newsflash (in small groups)

Act out or video a television news report with an interview and/or newspaper report with the four lovers (or Bottom), on romance and marriage, and their strange experiences in the woods. Create two reports: one in the style of a popular newspaper that prints scandal, and the other in the style of a serious newspaper.

4 The ballad of 'Bottom's Dream' (in large groups)

Write and perform your own version of this ballad as described in lines 206–11.

---

patched fool
  a fool wearing a patched coat
ballad a simple song

Peradventure perhaps
her death referring to Thisbe in
  the Mechanicals' play

DEMETRIUS These things seem small and undistinguishable,
　　　　Like far-off mountains turnèd into clouds.　　　　185
HERMIA Methinks I see these things with parted eye,
　　　　When everything seems double.
HELENA　　　　　　　　　　　So methinks;
　　　　And I have found Demetrius, like a jewel,
　　　　Mine own, and not mine own.
DEMETRIUS　　　　　　　　　Are you sure
　　　　That we are awake? It seems to me　　　　190
　　　　That yet we sleep, we dream. Do not you think
　　　　The Duke was here, and bid us follow him?
HERMIA Yea, and my father.
HELENA　　　　　　And Hippolyta.
LYSANDER And he did bid us follow to the temple.
DEMETRIUS Why, then, we are awake. Let's follow him,　　　　195
　　　　And by the way let us recount our dreams.

Exeunt lovers

Bottom wakes.

BOTTOM When my cue comes, call me, and I will answer. My next is
　　'Most fair Pyramus'. Heigh ho! Peter Quince? Flute the bellows-
　　mender? Snout the tinker? Starveling? God's my life! Stolen hence
　　and left me asleep! I have had a most rare vision. I have had a dream,　200
　　past the wit of man to say what dream it was. Man is but an ass
　　if he go about to expound this dream. Methought I was – there is
　　no man can tell what. Methought I was – and methought I had – but
　　man is but a patched fool if he will offer to say what methought
　　I had. The eye of man hath not heard, the ear of man hath not seen,　205
　　man's hand is not able to taste, his tongue to conceive, nor his heart
　　to report what my dream was! I will get Peter Quince to write a
　　ballad of this dream; it shall be called 'Bottom's Dream', because
　　it hath no bottom; and I will sing it in the latter end of a play, before
　　the Duke. Peradventure, to make it the more gracious, I shall sing　210
　　it at her death.　　　　　　　　　　　　　　　　　　　*Exit*

The Mechanicals, without Bottom, despair (they had been looking forward to a regular salary from the duke for their work); but Bottom suddenly arrives with the news that their play has been chosen.

1 A team?

Talk together about what sort of relationship the Mechanicals seem to have in the production shown above. Go on to discuss whether or not you feel they work well together as a team, giving evidence from the play.

transported carried away	**made men**
discharge perform	our fortunes would be made
paramour … thing of naught	**pumps** shoes
a mistress and, to Flute, something	**presently** immediately
immoral and wicked	**preferred** recommended for
	performance

ACT 4   SCENE 2
Athens

Enter QUINCE, FLUTE, SNOUT and STARVELING

QUINCE Have you sent to Bottom's house? Is he come home yet?

STARVELING He cannot be heard of. Out of doubt he is transported.

FLUTE If he come not, then the play is marred. It goes not forward. Doth it?

QUINCE It is not possible. You have not a man in all Athens able to 5 discharge Pyramus but he.

FLUTE No, he hath simply the best wit of any handicraft man in Athens.

QUINCE Yea, and the best person, too; and he is a very paramour for a sweet voice.

FLUTE You must say 'paragon'. A paramour is (God bless us!) a thing 10 of naught.   *Enter* SNUG *the joiner*

SNUG Masters, the Duke is coming from the temple, and there is two or three lords and ladies more married. If our sport had gone forward, we had all been made men.

FLUTE O, sweet bully Bottom! Thus hath he lost sixpence a day during 15 his life: he could not have 'scaped sixpence a day. And the Duke had not given him sixpence a day for playing Pyramus, I'll be hanged. He would have deserved it. Sixpence a day in Pyramus, or nothing.   *Enter* BOTTOM

BOTTOM Where are these lads? Where are these hearts? 20

QUINCE Bottom! O most courageous day! O most happy hour!

BOTTOM Masters, I am to discourse wonders – but ask me not what; for if I tell you, I am not true Athenian. I will tell you everything, right as it fell out.

QUINCE Let us hear, sweet Bottom. 25

BOTTOM Not a word of me. All that I will tell you is – that the Duke hath dined. Get your apparel together, good strings to your beards, new ribbons to your pumps: meet presently at the palace, every man look o'er his part. For the short and the long is, our play is preferred. In any case, let Thisbe have clean linen; and let not him that plays 30 the lion pare his nails, for they shall hang out for the lion's claws. And, most dear actors, eat no onions nor garlic; for we are to utter sweet breath, and I do not doubt but to hear them say it is a sweet comedy. No more words. Away! Go, away!   *Exeunt*

Looking back at Act 4
Activities for groups or individuals

1 'We are awake'

The dream part of the play now seems over, and the action returns the characters and audience to the 'real', daytime world. Discuss what the 'dream world' (or fantasy world) of Acts 2, 3 and 4 was like, comparing it with the everyday world of Athens in Act 1.

2 Making sense of it all?

It is often important to differentiate between dreams and reality. The lovers and Bottom attempt, in vain, to distinguish clearly between reality and imagination. Just how do you make sense of a dream? Bottom says that it is 'past the wit of man to say what dream it was', but many people believe that it is possible to make sense of dreams, that every dream has significance and meaning for the dreamer. Work in pairs, one person as Bottom, the other as a psychiatrist who interprets dreams. Bottom recounts the different experiences of his dream, and asks 'What does it all mean?' The psychiatrist explains.

3 Shakespeare's imagination

Shakespeare has just presented a complex 'dream world' which raises many questions. Here are some to start your discussion: What does each group of characters believe about this dream world? What do you make of it? Who's imagination is at work here: the characters', Shakespeare's or the audience's? What do you think Shakespeare might have had in mind when he created *A Midsummer Night's Dream*?

4 My story

In Scene 1, Theseus asks to hear the lovers' story soon ('we more will hear anon', line 175). Demetrius says they will 'recount our dreams' (line 196). Step into role as one of the lovers and tell your story.

5 Fairies

'The minute you say "fairy" to people, they think they know exactly what it is...'

This is what an actor who played a fairy in *A Midsummer Night's Dream* once said. Discuss the possibilities:

- Fairies at the bottom of the garden. The film *Fairy Stories* is a brilliant example of this (it is based on the true story of two young girls who claimed to see real fairies).
- Non-human spirits.
- A way of bringing on stage the world of fantasy and imagination.
- Representatives of magical and spiritual forces in human lives.

To help you think about this, look at the illustrations on pages 30, 36, 42, 44, 54, 74, 100 and 102. Also consider the fairies' names, and look at what they do in the play. Present your conclusions to the class.

6 Celebrity stories

The gossip columns would be having a field day with so many weddings. Write a few magazine/newspaper gossip stories based on the events of the play. Think about the key questions: What kind of background details would journalists be interested in? Who would they want a quote from? Have they got wind of the strange night in the woods?

How about a *Hello* or *National Enquirer* type scoop on the weddings?

7 Inside your head

Do you feel you are getting to know the characters more fully? Choose one character. Draw the character and ensure that you can lift up the head – like a pop-up book! Inside the head, write some of the character's thoughts. When the work of the whole class is put together, it makes a great display.

8 A fifty-word summary

Write an account of what happens in Act 4 in exactly fifty words.

Theseus and Hippolyta talk about the lovers' story,
and the power of imagination in poet, lover and madman,
who all see things that are not there.

1 Theseus versus Hippolyta (in pairs)

Taking a part each, read the speeches on the page opposite. Then compare their two judgements of the 'story of the night' and what it says about each character.

2 Do you believe in fairies? (I) (full-class debate)

Even in Shakespeare's day, belief in fairies wasn't the norm for educated people. Debate the statement, 'Ghosts, poltergeists and all things supernatural exist only in the imagination'.

3 Do you believe in fairies (II) (in groups of four)

Many people think that the fairies in this play represent what might be called a 'magical' or 'spiritual' side of our life, or even the power of imagination. Discuss how three types of people might react to seeing *A Midsummer Night's Dream* and its fairies – a Mechanicals-type person (a worker), a lover (a teenager in love) and a ruler like Theseus (a politician). Then improvise a scene of these three people leaving the theatre being interviewed about the play and what they thought of it.

4 *A Midsummer Night's Dream* itself (in pairs)

Theseus speaks of the imagination of a number of kinds of people, including 'the poet'. Read the description of what the poet does (lines 12–17), and discuss whether you think it describes *A Midsummer Night's Dream* itself. Go on to examine what part the imaginations of 'lovers' and 'lunatics' have in the play.

---

toys tales
seething agitated
compact composed

Helen Helen of Troy
(a famous beauty)
bodies forth creates
constancy certainty

ACT 5 SCENE I
Athens Theseus' Palace

Enter THESEUS, HIPPOLYTA, PHILOSTRATE, Lords and Attendants

HIPPOLYTA 'Tis strange, my Theseus, that these lovers speak of.
THESEUS More strange than true. I never may believe
These antique fables, nor these fairy toys.
Lovers and madmen have such seething brains,
Such shaping fantasies, that apprehend   5
More than cool reason ever comprehends.
The lunatic, the lover, and the poet
Are of imagination all compact:
One sees more devils than vast hell can hold;
That is the madman. The lover, all as frantic,   10
Sees Helen's beauty in a brow of Egypt.
The poet's eye, in a fine frenzy rolling,
Doth glance from heaven to earth, from earth to heaven;
And as imagination bodies forth
The forms of things unknown, the poet's pen   15
Turns them to shapes, and gives to airy nothing
A local habitation and a name.
Such tricks hath strong imagination
That if it would but apprehend some joy,
It comprehends some bringer of that joy;   20
Or in the night, imagining some fear,
How easy is a bush supposed a bear?
HIPPOLYTA But all the story of the night told over,
And all their minds transfigured so together,
More witnesseth than fancy's images,   25
And grows to something of great constancy;
But howsoever, strange and admirable.

The lovers enter, and Theseus looks through the list of performances ready for the evening's entertainment. He rejects the first three, but is attracted by the play of Pyramus and Thisbe.

The stage audience: the lovers wait for the entertainment.

masques dances or entertainments where masks were worn
abridgement pastime; to make time go quickly
beguile cheat
brief a summary
eunuch castrated man
tipsy Bacchanals drunken women (from Greek mythology)
device entertainment
Muses goddesses of learning and art
Not sorting with not appropriate to
concord harmony

Enter the lovers: LYSANDER, DEMETRIUS, HERMIA *and* HELENA

THESEUS Here come the lovers, full of joy and mirth.
　　　　Joy, gentle friends, joy and fresh days of love
　　　　Accompany your hearts!
LYSANDER　　　　　　　　　　More than to us 　　　　　　30
　　　　Wait in your royal walks, your board, your bed!
THESEUS Come now: what masques, what dances shall we have
　　　　To wear away this long age of three hours
　　　　Between our after-supper and bedtime?
　　　　Where is our usual manager of mirth? 　　　　　　35
　　　　What revels are in hand? Is there no play
　　　　To ease the anguish of a torturing hour?
　　　　Call Philostrate.
PHILOSTRATE　　　　　　　　Here, mighty Theseus.
THESEUS Say, what abridgement have you for this evening?
　　　　What masque, what music? How shall we beguile 　　40
　　　　The lazy time if not with some delight?
PHILOSTRATE [*Giving him a paper.*]
　　　　There is a brief how many sports are ripe.
　　　　Make choice of which your highness will see first.
THESEUS [*Reading.*]
　　　　'The battle with the Centaurs, to be sung
　　　　By an Athenian eunuch to the harp' – 　　　　　　45
　　　　We'll none of that; that have I told my love
　　　　In glory of my kinsman, Hercules.
　　　　[*Reading.*] 'The riot of the tipsy Bacchanals,
　　　　Tearing the Thracian singer in their rage' –
　　　　That is an old device, and it was played 　　　　　50
　　　　When I from Thebes came last a conqueror.
　　　　[*Reading.*] 'The thrice three Muses mourning for the death
　　　　Of learning, late deceased in beggary' –
　　　　That is some satire keen and critical,
　　　　Not sorting with a nuptial ceremony. 　　　　　　55
　　　　[*Reading.*] 'A tedious brief scene of young Pyramus
　　　　And his love Thisbe, very tragical mirth' –
　　　　Merry and tragical? Tedious and brief?
　　　　That is hot ice and wondrous strange snow!
　　　　How shall we find the concord of this discord? 　　60

Theseus decides on the Mechanicals' play despite the objections of Philostrate, who says the rehearsal was laughably bad.

---

1 Is Philostrate being fair? (in groups of four)

Examine Philostrate's description of the Mechanicals and their play, and consider whether you think he is being fair to them.

2 Audience one, audience two (in groups of four)

The Mechanicals will perform to two audiences: the court, and the audience watching *A Midsummer Night's Dream*. The audience gets an outsider's view of the Mechanicals' play here – look at Philostrate's description (lines 61–70), and try to think of reasons why Shakespeare included this description of the play when both audiences were about to see it anyway. Do you think that both audiences will react in the same way to the Mechanicals' play? Report back to the class on your conclusions.

3 Seeing the play on 29 September 1662

Samuel Pepys saw the play on this date and wrote:

> 'and then to the King's Theatre, where we saw *Midsummer Night's Dreame*, which I have never seen before, nor shall ever again, for it is the most insipid ridiculous play that I ever saw in my life.'

Do you think this fits the Mechanicals' play better than the whole play? Write down your reasons.

4 Hippolyta's response

How does Hippolyta speak lines 85–6? What do these lines reveal about her?

---

toiled work until weary
unbreathed unpractised
sport fun, entertainment
conned learnt

wretchedness o'ercharged
those of little ability overstretched
(or poor people made mock of)

PHILOSTRATE A play there is, my lord, some ten words long,
    Which is as 'brief' as I have known a play,
    But by ten words, my lord, it is too long,
    Which makes it 'tedious'. For in all the play
    There is not one word apt, one player fitted.   65
    And 'tragical', my noble lord, it is,
    For Pyramus therein doth kill himself,
    Which when I saw rehearsed, I must confess,
    Made mine eyes water; but more 'merry' tears
    The passion of loud laughter never shed.   70
THESEUS What are they that do play it?
PHILOSTRATE Hard-handed men that work in Athens here,
    Which never laboured in their minds till now;
    And now have toiled their unbreathed memories
    With this same play against your nuptial.   75
THESEUS And we will hear it.
PHILOSTRATE   No, my noble lord,
    It is not for you. I have heard it over,
    And it is nothing, nothing in the world,
    Unless you can find sport in their intents,
    Extremely stretched, and conned with cruel pain,   80
    To do you service.
THESEUS   I will hear that play;
    For never anything can be amiss
    When simpleness and duty tender it.
    Go bring them in; and take your places, ladies.
                        [*Exit Philostrate*]
HIPPOLYTA I love not to see wretchedness o'ercharged,   85
    And duty in his service perishing.
THESEUS Why, gentle sweet, you shall see no such thing.
HIPPOLYTA He says they can do nothing in this kind.

Theseus explains his choice of the Mechanicals' play: it is the thought that counts among simple people. Quince then enters and begins the play, rather strangely.

1 On show (in small groups)

We are all on show to others every time we are in public. But great occasions can stop us speaking altogether. In lines 93–105, Theseus talks about learned people such as 'great clerks' being unable to talk during official welcomes. He also criticises 'audacious eloquence', those who speak perhaps a little too well in public. He seems to prefer 'love' (in the wider sense of deep affection) and 'tongue-tied simplicity', those who speak a little ('least') but communicate a great deal ('speak most'). Describe occasions when you as individuals have had to speak in public or have been intimidated by a group or person.

2 Well said! (in pairs)

Quince's Prologue (lines 108–17) has much of its punctuation in the wrong place (that's why the court jokes about his 'points' and 'stops' – the punctuation). One person practise the speech as it is written (bearing in mind what the audience says), and the other try to re-punctuate the speech to make better sense. Then speak the two versions one after another – which works best?

3 Asides: does Quince hear? (in groups of four)

Discuss whether Quince hears the comments of the court (lines 118–23), or whether they are asides (heard only by the audience). Try acting it out both ways: if Quince hears, he will react; if he doesn't, he will have to be doing something – even if only standing still. Keep this in mind for the rest of the Mechanicals' play.

---

in might, not merit
  accepts it given the ability of those
  that offer it
premeditated welcomes
  planned speeches
periods stops
capacity understanding

addressed ready
stand upon points
  take notice of punctuation or detail
stop a pun on full stop, and
  suddenly stopping a horse when
  riding
in government under control

THESEUS The kinder we, to give them thanks for nothing.
     Our sport shall be to take what they mistake; 90
     And what poor duty cannot do, noble respect
     Takes it in might, not merit.
     Where I have come, great clerks have purposèd
     To greet me with premeditated welcomes,
     Where I have seen them shiver and look pale, 95
     Make periods in the midst of sentences,
     Throttle their practised accent in their fears,
     And in conclusion dumbly have broke off,
     Not paying me a welcome. Trust me, sweet,
     Out of this silence yet I picked a welcome, 100
     And in the modesty of fearful duty
     I read as much as from the rattling tongue
     Of saucy and audacious eloquence.
     Love, therefore, and tongue-tied simplicity
     In least speak most, to my capacity. 105

Enter PHILOSTRATE

PHILOSTRATE So please your grace, the Prologue is addressed.
THESEUS Let him approach.

Flourish of trumpets.

Enter QUINCE *as Prologue*

QUINCE   If we offend, it is with our good will.
       That you should think, we come not to offend,
     But with good will. To show our simple skill, 110
       That is the true beginning of our end.
     Consider then, we come but in despite.
       We do not come as minding to content you,
     Our true intent is. All for your delight,
       We are not here. That you should here repent you, 115
     The actors are at hand; and by their show
     You shall know all that you are like to know.
THESEUS This fellow doth not stand upon points.
LYSANDER He hath rid his prologue like a rough colt; he knows not
    the stop. A good moral, my lord; it is not enough to speak, but to 120
    speak true.
HIPPOLYTA Indeed, he hath played on this prologue like a child on
    a recorder – a sound, but not in government.

Quince continues with the Prologue, which explains the play, and introduces the characters.

1 Getting on and off (in groups of six)

At the beginning of the Prologue all the Mechanicals come on to the stage and all but Snout exit at the end of it. How would you have them do this? Would you, for example, have a noisy and messy entrance, or a more subdued and humble approach? Try out a few ideas.

2 Mime to the Prologue

Mime along with the Prologue (spoken by the person playing Quince), developing each character's actions and reactions. Try different ways of doing this: completely over the top, stumbling and muddled, or in any other way which you think might work. Choose your favourite version and present it to the class.

3 The play itself (in small groups)

Using the Prologue, discuss what kind of play it is, how it is described by Quince, and what this tells you about the Mechanicals and their ideas about what a play should be.

4 A quick thought

Compare this speech (lines 126–50) to Quince's previous one (lines 108–117). Think about how they are different – and why.

---

sunder keep apart
lanthorn lantern
hight is called
mantle cloak
fall let fall

Anon soon
broached stabbed
tarrying waiting
twain two

THESEUS His speech was like a tangled chain, nothing impaired, but
all disordered. Who is next?   125

Enter with a Trumpeter before them [BOTTOM *as*] *Pyramus,* [FLUTE *as*]
Thisbe, [SNOUT *as*] *Wall,* [STARVELING *as*] *Moonshine and* [SNUG *as*]
Lion.

QUINCE (*as Prologue*)
      Gentles, perchance you wonder at this show,
        But wonder on, till truth make all things plain.
      This man is Pyramus, if you would know;
        This beauteous lady Thisbe is, certain.
      This man with lime and rough-cast doth present   130
        Wall, that vile wall which did these lovers sunder;
      And through Wall's chink, poor souls, they are content
        To whisper – at the which let no man wonder.
      This man with lanthorn, dog, and bush of thorn,
        Presenteth Moonshine; for, if you will know,   135
      By moonshine did these lovers think no scorn
        To meet at Ninus' tomb, there, there to woo.
      This grisly beast, which Lion hight by name,
      The trusty Thisbe, coming first by night,
      Did scare away, or rather did affright;   140
      And as she fled, her mantle she did fall,
        Which Lion vile with bloody mouth did stain.
      Anon comes Pyramus, sweet youth and tall,
        And finds his trusty Thisbe's mantle slain;
      Whereat with blade, with bloody, blameful blade,   145
        He bravely broached his boiling bloody breast;
      And Thisbe, tarrying in mulberry shade,
        His dagger drew, and died. For all the rest,
      Let Lion, Moonshine, Wall, and lovers twain
      At large discourse, while here they do remain.   150
          Exeunt Quince, Bottom, Flute, Snug and Starveling

Snout, as the Wall, explains his role.
Bottom, as Pyramus, enters and begins the play's action.

---

1 Bottom's up (in pairs)

Everyone needs to have a chance to be Bottom — take turns acting out his speech (lines 168–78) – your partner can be the admiring Wall.

2 O speech, O speech so full of Os (in pairs)

Have a close look at Bottom's speech and all the repetitions of words and ideas. Think of some way of showing these repetitions, either by emphasising them as you speak the lines, or in some kind of written display work.

3 O speech beyond compare (in pairs)

Compare Bottom's lines 167–78 to Snout's lines 153–62. Write down the differences, and what they suggest about each character.

4 Did you say something? (in pairs)

What do you make of what is going on in lines 179–82? Try different ways of acting them out (perhaps starting with the last four lines of Bottom's speech as Pyramus).

5 Social class issues?

Comments made about the players and the play show the attitude the court has to the Mechanicals' play. What class issues could be raised through the way in which those remarks are spoken?

---

interlude short play
sinister left
partition wall
  (or section of a speech)

curse again should curse back,
  since it is 'sensible' (alive)
fall pat come right

THESEUS I wonder if the lion be to speak?
DEMETRIUS No wonder, my lord; one lion may, when many asses do.
SNOUT (*as Wall*)

> In this same interlude it doth befall
> That I, one Snout by name, present a wall;
> And such a wall as I would have you think   155
> That had in it a crannied hole or chink,
> Through which the lovers, Pyramus and Thisbe,
> Did whisper often, very secretly.
> This loam, this rough-cast, and this stone doth show
> That I am that same wall; the truth is so.   160
> And this the cranny is, right and sinister,
> Through which the fearful lovers are to whisper.

THESEUS Would you desire lime and hair to speak better?
DEMETRIUS It is the wittiest partition that ever I heard discourse, my
  lord.   165

Enter BOTTOM *as* PYRAMUS

THESEUS Pyramus draws near the wall; silence!
BOTTOM (*as Pyramus*)

> O grim-looked night, O night with hue so black,
>   O night which ever art when day is not!
> O night, O night, alack, alack, alack,
>   I fear my Thisbe's promise is forgot!   170
> And thou, O wall, O sweet, O lovely wall,
>   That stand'st between her father's ground and mine,
> Thou wall, O wall, O sweet and lovely wall,
>   Show me thy chink, to blink through with mine eyne.
>   [*Wall parts his fingers.*]
> Thanks, courteous wall; Jove shield thee well for this!   175
>   But what see I? No Thisbe do I see.
> O wicked wall, through whom I see no bliss,
>   Cursed be thy stones for thus deceiving me!

THESEUS The wall, methinks, being sensible, should curse again.
BOTTOM No, in truth sir, he should not. 'Deceiving me' is Thisbe's   180
  cue. She is to enter now, and I am to spy her through the wall.
  You shall see it will fall pat as I told you. Yonder she comes.

Thisbe and Pyramus declare their love for each other through the chink in the wall, and agree to meet at 'Ninny's tomb'.

1 Gooseberry (in groups of three)

Start by looking at Flute's speeches opposite, thinking about 'her' voice and actions. Talk about Bottom's speeches, then the gooseberry, or overhearer: Snout as Wall, and how he is reacting to the other two. Finally, get up and act different ways of performing the lines.

Limander, Helen
  this should be Leander and Hero,
  two legendary lovers
Fates see page 136
	Shafalus, Procrus this should be
	  Cephalus and Procris, other
	  legendary lovers
	Tide come

Enter FLUTE *as* THISBE

FLUTE (*as Thisbe*)
>O wall, full often hast thou heard my moans,
>>For parting my fair Pyramus and me.
>My cherry lips have often kissed thy stones,   185
>>Thy stones with lime and hair knit up in thee.

BOTTOM (*as Pyramus*)
>I see a voice; now will I to the chink,
>>To spy and I can hear my Thisbe's face.
>Thisbe!

FLUTE (*as Thisbe*)
>>>>>My love! Thou art my love, I think?

BOTTOM (*as Pyramus*)
>Think what thou wilt, I am thy lover's grace,   190
>And like Limander am I trusty still.

FLUTE (*as Thisbe*)
>And I like Helen, till the Fates me kill.

BOTTOM (*as Pyramus*)
>Not Shafalus to Procrus was so true.

FLUTE (*as Thisbe*)
>As Shafalus to Procrus, I to you.

BOTTOM (*as Pyramus*)
>O, kiss me through the hole of this vile wall!   195

FLUTE (*as Thisbe*)
>I kiss the wall's hole, not your lips at all.

BOTTOM (*as Pyramus*)
>Wilt thou at Ninny's tomb meet me straightway?

FLUTE (*as Thisbe*)
>Tide life, tide death, I come without delay.
>>>>>[*Exeunt Bottom and Flute in different directions*]

The stage audience comments on the play,
and Snug (the lion) enters, explaining he is not really a lion.

1 Give each line its due (in small groups)

Hippolyta says 'This is the silliest stuff that ever I heard' – do you agree? Compare her comment with what Samuel Pepys said (page 122). Theseus replies 'The best in this kind are but shadows' – what might he mean? Talk about what Theseus says in lines 205–10 and whether you agree with him. Share your conclusions on all these points with the class.

mural wall	**fox … goose**
wilful ready	the lion was supposed to be brave,
fell fierce	the fox cunning ('discretion') and
dam mother (lioness)	the goose stupid

SNOUT (*as Wall*)
>Thus have I, Wall, my part dischargèd so;
>And being done, thus Wall away doth go.   *Exit*   200

THESEUS Now is the mural down between the two neighbours.

DEMETRIUS No remedy, my lord, when walls are so wilful to hear without warning.

HIPPOLYTA This is the silliest stuff that ever I heard.

THESEUS The best in this kind are but shadows; and the worst are no   205
worse, if imagination amend them.

HIPPOLYTA It must be your imagination then, and not theirs.

THESEUS If we imagine no worse of them than they of themselves, they
may pass for excellent men. Here come two noble beasts in, a man
and a lion.   210

Enter [Snug as] Lion and [Starveling as] Moonshine.

SNUG (*as Lion*)
>You ladies, you whose gentle hearts do fear
>>The smallest monstrous mouse that creeps on floor,
>May now, perchance, both quake and tremble here,
>>When Lion rough in wildest rage doth roar.
>Then know that I as Snug the joiner am   215
>A lion fell, nor else no lion's dam;
>For if I should as lion come in strife
>Into this place, 'twere pity on my life.

THESEUS A very gentle beast, and of a good conscience.

DEMETRIUS The very best at a beast, my lord, that e'er I saw.   220

LYSANDER This lion is a very fox for his valour.

THESEUS True; and a goose for his discretion.

DEMETRIUS Not so, my lord; for his valour cannot carry his discretion;
and the fox carries the goose.

THESEUS His discretion, I am sure, cannot carry his valour; for the   225
goose carries not the fox. It is well: leave it to his discretion, and
let us listen to the moon.

*Starveling, as the Moon, manages to explain his role,
despite the comments of the stage audience.
Thisbe arrives only to be frightened away by the lion.*

1 The unruly audience (in groups of six to eight)

The stage audience seems to be getting out of hand. Taking parts, read through lines 228–55 a couple of times. Come to some conclusions about Starveling seeming to give up on speaking his lines, and on how the audience is behaving. Think about the end of this section, where the audience seems to be shouting out ironic comments like a football crowd. Try different ways to bring all this out when you act it, and then show your version to the class.

2 Imagining the moon (in small groups)

The image of the moon is common throughout *A Midsummer Night's Dream*. Find some earlier references to the moon and compare them with the presentation of the moon opposite. You might like to discuss the differences between what the audience are asked to do in the whole play (imagine both the moon and its effects from just Shakespeare's words), and what the Mechanicals think their audience needs. Perhaps the Mechanicals look down on the understanding and imagination of their audience, just as their audience looks down on them. Discuss some ideas of how the court or the lovers or both would have presented the story of Pyramus and Thisbe. Improvise a small part of such a play, and show it to the class.

---

horns on his head the sign of a cuckold (someone whose wife has been unfaithful)
crescent waxing moon (growing larger)

already in snuff already snuffed out
Well moused the lion is like a cat with a mouse (the mantle)

STARVELING (*as Moonshine*)
> This lanthorn doth the hornèd moon present –

DEMETRIUS He should have worn the horns on his head.

THESEUS He is no crescent, and his horns are invisible within the   230
circumference.

STARVELING (*as Moonshine*)
> This lanthorn doth the hornèd moon present;
> Myself the man i'th'moon do seem to be –

THESEUS This is the greatest error of all the rest; the man should be
put into the lantern. How is it else the man i'th'moon?   235

DEMETRIUS He dares not come there, for the candle; for you see it is
already in snuff.

HIPPOLYTA I am aweary of this moon. Would he would change!

THESEUS It appears by his small light of discretion that he is in the
wane; but yet in courtesy, in all reason, we must stay the time.   240

LYSANDER Proceed, Moon.

STARVELING All that I have to say is to tell you that the lanthorn is
the moon, I the man i'th'moon, this thorn bush my thorn bush,
and this dog my dog.

DEMETRIUS Why, all these should be in the lantern, for all these are   245
in the moon. But silence: here comes Thisbe.

Enter [FLUTE *as*] THISBE

FLUTE (*as Thisbe*)
> This is old Ninny's tomb. Where is my love?

SNUG (*as Lion*) O!

Lion roars. Thisbe runs off [*dropping her mantle*]

DEMETRIUS Well roared, Lion!

THESEUS Well run, Thisbe!   250

HIPPOLYTA Well shone, Moon! Truly, the moon shines with a good
grace.

THESEUS Well moused, Lion!

DEMETRIUS And then came Pyramus –

LYSANDER And so the lion vanished.   255

[Lion worries Thisbe's mantle, and exit]

Pyramus enters full of expectation.
He then sees Thisbe's blood-stained mantle, and calls
for his own death.

---

1 Bottom as an actor (in small groups)

Read the comments on Bottom's acting (lines 272–4). Use the remarks to compare Bottom as an actor and Bottom as a character and the relationship between the two.

2 Every trick in the book (in pairs)

Start by reading Bottom's lines 256–71 to each other. Then consider the speech again as if you were Shakespeare, thinking about what you've put in to make Bottom appear ridiculous. Make a list of such 'tricks' of language and rhyme, explaining if you can what sort of 'tricks' they are (the activities on page 128 can help to get you started). One of you present your ideas to the class as if you were Shakespeare. It should be possible to have a class full of Shakespeares discussing the ideas they had while writing the speech, how successful they feel they were and how they envisage an actor speaking and acting it.

3 Romeo and Juliet – a parody?

As you work through the Mechanicals' play, keep thinking about whether Shakespeare is mocking his own *Romeo and Juliet*. Watch for similarities.

---

dole reason for sadness
Furies avenging goddesses
Fates, thread and thrum
  the goddesses controlling lives,
  spinning out the threads of
  people's lives, and ending them by
  cutting the thread and thrum (tuft
  on a thread)

Quail destroy
quell kill
Beshrew my heart exclamation,
  like 'Bless my soul'

Enter BOTTOM *as* PYRAMUS

BOTTOM (*as Pyramus*)
       Sweet moon, I thank thee for thy sunny beams;
        I thank thee, moon, for shining now so bright;
      For by thy gracious, golden, glittering gleams
        I trust to take of truest Thisbe sight.
            But stay – O spite! 260
            But mark, poor Knight,
          What dreadful dole is here?
            Eyes, do you see?
            How can it be?
          O dainty duck, O dear! 265
            Thy mantle good –
          What, stained with blood?
          Approach, ye Furies fell!
            O Fates, come, come,
            Cut thread and thrum, 270
         Quail, crush, conclude, and quell.
THESEUS This passion, and the death of a dear friend, would go near
    to make a man look sad.
HIPPOLYTA Beshrew my heart, but I pity the man.

Pyramus stabs himself, and has a prolonged death.
As the audience comments on the acting, Thisbe enters.

---

1 A good-looking girl, that Thisbe

Take a look at the man playing Flute (Thisbe) in the photograph on page 140. Think about whether you like the image he puts across, and what Flute might be like if played by other very different looking actors. The actor on page 130, for example, is much more feminine looking.

2 *Shakespeare in Love*: the movie

The film *Shakespeare in Love* deals very creatively with the concept of women on the stage in Elizabethan England. This film provides an enjoyable background to the study of Shakespeare's plays. If you have seen it, what does it add to your understanding of *A Midsummer Night's Dream*?

3 An ass by any other name ... (in small groups)

Yet again, someone implies that Bottom is an 'ass' (line 294). With a name like Bottom, and having an ass' head at one point, this idea of his character is pretty clear. Think about what Bottom says and does throughout the play, and make a list of reasons why Bottom is – or isn't – an ass.

---

deflowered wasted
pap breast
die (line 291) one of a pair of dice; and ace (one) is the lowest throw (Demetrius puns on Bottom's use of 'die')

mote tiny particle
balance scale
means, videlicet moans, makes a formal legal complaint

BOTTOM (*as Pyramus*)
    O wherefore, Nature, didst thou lions frame,   275
      Since lion vile hath here deflowered my dear?
    Which is – no, no – which was the fairest dame
      That lived, that loved, that liked, that looked with cheer.
        Come tears, confound!
        Out sword, and wound   280
      The pap of Pyramus,
        Ay, that left pap,
        Where heart doth hop:
      Thus die I, thus, thus, thus! [*Stabs himself.*]
        Now am I dead,   285
        Now am I fled;
      My soul is in the sky.
        Tongue, lose thy light;
        Moon, take thy flight;
                         [*Exit Starveling*]
      Now die, die, die, die, die. [*He dies.*]   290
DEMETRIUS No die, but an ace for him; for he is but one.
LYSANDER Less than an ace, man; for he is dead, he is nothing.
THESEUS With the help of a surgeon he might yet recover, and yet prove
   an ass.
HIPPOLYTA How chance Moonshine is gone before Thisbe comes back 295
   and finds her lover?
THESEUS She will find him by starlight.

            Enter [FLUTE *as*] THISBE

    Here she comes and her passion ends the play.
HIPPOLYTA Methinks she should not use a long one for such a
   Pyramus; I hope she will be brief.   300
DEMETRIUS A mote will turn the balance, which Pyramus, which
   Thisbe is the better: he for a man, God warrant us; she for a woman,
   God bless us.
LYSANDER She hath spied him already, with those sweet eyes.
DEMETRIUS And thus she means, videlicet –   305

Thisbe realises Pyramus is dead and kills herself.
Bottom asks if the duke wants an epilogue or a dance.
Theseus settles on the country dance.

The Mechanicals' play. Act out your own version of Bottom's
and Flute's final speeches (lines 275–90 and lines 306–29).
Make the most of any ridiculous images and lines, such as Bottom's
'Now die, die, die, die, die'.

2 'Your play needs no excuse' (in small groups)

Discuss whether the Mechanicals' play needs excusing (line 335),
and then look again at the plays Theseus had a choice of viewing
(lines 44–60). Decide whether Theseus' choice was wise, bearing in
mind how the audience reacted to the Mechanicals' play. Report
back to the rest of the class with your conclusions.

sisters three the Fates	**imbrue** stab, make bloody
(see the gloss on page 136)	**notably discharged**
gore blood	admirably performed
shore cut	**Bergomask** a country dance
thread of silk life-line	

FLUTE (*as Thisbe*)

        Asleep, my love?
        What, dead, my dove?
    O Pyramus, arise.
        Speak, speak! Quite dumb?
        Dead, dead? A tomb   310
    Must cover thy sweet eyes.
        These lily lips,
        This cherry nose,
    These yellow cowslip cheeks
        Are gone, are gone.   315
        Lovers, make moan;
    His eyes were green as leeks.
        O sisters three,
        Come, come to me
    With hands as pale as milk;   320
        Lay them in gore,
        Since you have shore
    With shears his thread of silk.
        Tongue, not a word!
        Come, trusty sword,   325
    Come blade, my breast imbrue! [*Stabs herself.*]
        And farewell, friends.
        Thus Thisbe ends –
    Adieu, adieu, adieu! [*Dies.*]

THESEUS Moonshine and Lion are left to bury the dead.   330

DEMETRIUS Ay, and Wall, too.

BOTTOM [*Starting up, as Flute does also.*] No, I assure you, the wall is down that parted their fathers. Will it please you to see the epilogue, or to hear a Bergomask dance between two of our company?

THESEUS No epilogue, I pray you; for your play needs no excuse. Never   335 excuse; for when the players are all dead, there need none to be blamed. Marry, if he that writ it had played Pyramus and hanged himself in Thisbe's garter, it would have been a fine tragedy: and so it is, truly, and very notably discharged. But come, your Bergomask; let your epilogue alone.   340

The Mechanicals dance, the duke instructs everyone to go to bed, and Puck enters. He speaks of the night, the time that the fairies play.

---

1 The dance (in groups of five)

It was quite common in Shakespeare's day for plays to end with a dance. The Bergomask was a country dance, but using any kind of music you think suitable, work out a dance for the Mechanicals.

2 Puck's world

Make an illustration of Puck's lines 349–69, based on the images in his speech. Again, Shakespeare invites the audience to imagine this visual scene. Write about the difference between your illustration and Puck's words. You could put different illustrations up on display.

3 A different mood? (in pairs)

One person read Theseus' speech, the other Puck's. Think carefully about differences between them, particularly in mood and images, and in the feel they give to the play. Read the two speeches again, this time with actions, trying to emphasise those differences between them (you may find some similarities). If you were directing the play, what would you do with the lighting during lines 348–9? Contrast Puck's world and the world of Theseus at this moment.

4 All together now: one, two, three … (in pairs)

Here the Mechanicals, the court and the fairies are in the same place in quick succession. How would the three groups look back on the events of the play?

---

iron tongue … told
  the bell was struck
overwatched watched over
palpable-gross obviously uncouth
heavy gait laboured passage,
  slow-moving pace

heavy (line 351) tired
foredone worn out
wasted brands burnt logs
triple Hecate's team
  the moon's chariot
hallowed saintly

[The company return; two of them dance, then exeunt Bottom, Flute and their fellows.]

The iron tongue of midnight hath told twelve.
Lovers, to bed; 'tis almost fairy time.
I fear we shall outsleep the coming morn
As much as we this night have overwatched.
This palpable-gross play hath well beguiled   345
The heavy gait of night. Sweet friends, to bed.
A fortnight hold we this solemnity
In nightly revels and new jollity.

Exeunt

Enter PUCK *[carrying a broom]*

PUCK   Now the hungry lion roars,
                    And the wolf behowls the moon,   350
                Whilst the heavy ploughman snores,
                    All with weary task foredone.
                Now the wasted brands do glow,
                    Whilst the screech-owl, screeching loud,
                Puts the wretch that lies in woe   355
                    In remembrance of a shroud.
                Now it is the time of night
                    That the graves, all gaping wide,
                Every one lets forth his sprite
                    In the church-way paths to glide.   360
                And we fairies, that do run
                    By the triple Hecate's team
                From the presence of the sun,
                    Following darkness like a dream,
                Now are frolic; not a mouse   365
                Shall disturb this hallowed house.
                I am sent with broom before
                To sweep the dust behind the door.

Oberon and Titania, with their fairies, enter, and Oberon instructs them to go through the house, blessing the three couples with loving marriages and 'perfect' children.

1 Watch your language

The lovers are upper class and the Mechanicals are workers – and Shakespeare makes their language very different. For the fairies, Shakespeare uses the language of country myths and certain kinds of literature. Write a modern blessing for couples about to marry in the manner of Oberon's lines 379–400. Compare it with Oberon's speech and a blessing from *The Book of Common Prayer* (1662) on marriage and children:

> We beseech thee, assist with thy blessing these two persons, that they may both be fruitful in procreation of children, and also live together so long in godly love and honesty, that they may see their children christianly and virtuously brought up, to thy praise and honour; through Jesus Christ our Lord.

2 The dance again (in groups of six or more)

Picking your own music, improvise and develop a dance (and song) to suit the fairies and the moment in the play.

3 'Sweet peace' (in groups of four to six)

Compare the speeches opposite with the conflicts of the opening scene and the conflicts in the wood, noting the differences. Everyone is now together in the same place (Theseus' palace), and the marriages are blessed. In the play, there are many problems in the relationships between women and men. What has brought them to 'sweet peace' now? For each couple, find explanations of how their problems have been resolved. Think about the spiritual or mental changes, as well as the way the plot works.

---

best bride-bed the wedding bed
of Theseus and Hippolyta
issue children

mark prodigious
birthmark with an evil omen
take his gait go his way

Enter [OBERON *and* TITANIA,] *the King and Queen of Fairies, with all their train.*

OBERON	Through the house give glimmering light
	By the dead and drowsy fire; 370
	Every elf and fairy sprite
	Hop as light as bird from briar,
	And this ditty after me
	Sing, and dance it trippingly.
TITANIA	First rehearse your song by rote, 375
	To each word a warbling note;
	Hand in hand with fairy grace
	Will we sing and bless this place.

Song [*and dance*].

OBERON	Now until the break of day
	Through this house each fairy stray. 380
	To the best bride-bed will we,
	Which by us shall blessèd be;
	And the issue there create
	Ever shall be fortunate.
	So shall all the couples three 385
	Ever true in loving be,
	And the blots of nature's hand
	Shall not in their issue stand.
	Never mole, harelip, nor scar,
	Nor mark prodigious, such as are 390
	Despisèd in nativity,
	Shall upon their children be.
	With this field-dew consecrate,
	Every fairy take his gait,
	And each several chamber bless 395
	Through this palace with sweet peace;
	And the owner of it blessed
	Ever shall in safety rest.
	Trip away, make no stay;
	Meet me all by break of day. 400

Exeunt [*all but Puck*]

Puck, on his own now, asks for the audience to think of the play as their dream. He promises improved performances and asks for the audience's approval.

---

1 Shakespeare's audience (in groups of four to six)

Shakespeare's audience would, apparently, either hiss ('the serpent's tongue') or clap ('Give me your hands') at the end of plays. Plays often ended with a request to the audience to clap (and not hiss!). Is Puck the right person to ask the audience for their applause, and the right person to end the play?

2 Exploring patterns (in pairs)

Look very closely at the words Puck uses in lines 401–8, and group his words into patterns ('shadows', 'slumbered', 'visions', 'dream' might be one). Relate these patterns to the play as a whole.

3 What are plays anyway? (in groups of four to six)

The Mechanicals have shown their play. *A Midsummer Night's Dream* ends with Shakespeare calling the actors 'shadows' (line 401) and the play itself 'visions'.

Discuss what you think plays (and films and drama on television) actually are, and why people still like to watch such 'visions' and 'dreams'.

4 Whose dream? (in groups of four to six)

The lovers and Bottom have already been involved in experiences that they think are dreams. Now Puck suggests the whole play is 'but a dream' for the audience. Whose 'dream' is the play – the audience's, Shakespeare's, the mortals in the play, all of these, or ...?

---

mend improve
'scape the serpent's tongue
  escape the audience hissing
  (because of a poor performance)

Give me your hands applaud
restore amends
  Puck will, in return, make amends

PUCK [*To the audience*]
> If we shadows have offended,
> Think but this, and all is mended:
> That you have but slumbered here
> While these visions did appear;
> And this weak and idle theme,   405
> No more yielding but a dream,
> Gentles, do not reprehend;
> If you pardon, we will mend.
> And, as I am an honest Puck,
> If we have unearnèd luck   410
> Now to 'scape the serpent's tongue
> We will make amends ere long,
> Else the Puck a liar call.
> So, good night unto you all.
> Give me your hands, if we be friends,   415
> And Robin shall restore amends.   [*Exit*]

Looking back at the play

Activities for groups or individuals

Images of Puck: compare this photograph of Puck with other images of
Puck in the script. Talk together about what you think are the good
and bad points of each, and decide how you would present Puck in
your own production of *A Midsummer Night's Dream*.

1 Puck – as symbol

'We cannot possibly deal with Puck as a realistic character.'

Say whether or not you agree with this statement, then suggest
what issues and themes Shakespeare is exploring through this
character or dramatic device. Brainstorm your ideas in a small
group in the form of a spider diagram.

2 Pyramus and Thisbe: the sequel

Think about the story of Pyramus and Thisbe, and pick a moment
the Mechanicals left out – say, when Pyramus and Thisbe's parents

hear of their deaths. Work together to write the speeches using Shakespeare's tricks to make it ridiculous. Display your script in the classroom, and act it out.

3 Different kinds of lovers

In Act 5 Scene 1, lines 191–4, Pyramus and Thisbe compare themselves to four famous lovers. Compare the lovers in the Mechanicals' play with the lovers in *A Midsummer Night's Dream*. Discuss whether young love should be treated seriously, or whether there can be a funny side to it – for outsiders.

4 The Mechanicals' play

Act out the whole of the Mechanicals' play (Act 5 Scene 1, lines 108–329) leaving out the comments of the audience. Concentrate on ways to make it as hilarious as possible. Have fun! Experiment with different genre: pantomime, farce or situation comedy, for example.

5 Authorial point

What do you think were Shakespeare's own views about the Mechanicals? You may or may not want to take into account the views of their court audience. You may also wish to reflect upon class, culture, education, humour, loyalty, society, patronage, respect, responsibility, and so on.

6 The dark side

Although this play falls firmly into the comedy category of Shakespearean plays, it does have its bleak and unpleasant moments and images. Analyse what you find particularly disturbing. Present your findings in pictorial or diagrammatic format.

7 The dark side: the future

You are a script writer commissioned by a famous Hollywood director to come up with a version of *A Midsummer Night's Dream* to be set in the future and modelled on the blockbuster films in the *Star Wars* series. In pairs, work on one short scene and come up with some suggestions to present at a script meeting which will be held tomorrow. You are under pressure to come up with some exciting ideas in a very short space of time.

A Midsummer Night's Dream in production

Starting points for class, group and individual work

'You don't do a play to neaten it up, to whip it into shape: you do it to release it, to unleash it from the page. It's up to you what to make of it.'

The view of an actor who played Titania and Hippolyta.

An ideal way to explore the play is to take part in a production of it. This would mean making many key decisions: where the play is set (ancient Athens? modern Grimsby?), how the fairies are to be presented, how the play should be cut (or should it be cut at all?), and similar issues. There are also a host of different jobs in a production: acting, lighting, costumes, front-of-house, and so on.

You could also try shorter versions of the play (or of parts of it). A useful approach is to put on a version of the play that lasts a very short time, perhaps twenty minutes. This could be done with a combination of mime, narration and dialogue from the play, and music and dance. You would need to develop a script first, and then work in groups on the different scenes. The final production could be to younger children, perhaps in their schools.

An even shorter version could be created by selecting some of the key speeches/lines/images in the play, and performing them as a group. You could combine choral (group) speaking, different parts being spoken by different people, and music. This would give an aural version of the play, though it could be combined with mime and/or tableaux (or still photographs). Perhaps the shortest of all would be tableaux of the four to six key moments in the play (as you see them). This is something you could easily do in the classroom.

As some of the activities suggest, with a comedy, it's often not what you do, but the way that you do it which is important. Experiments with different ways of acting out any part of the play, or trying out various interpretations of a character are valuable ways of exploring the play. Your group can pick its own section of the play (or a character) and experiment with how the humour can be brought out.

The fairy problem

'The minute you say "fairy" to people, they think they know exactly what it is – and they're outraged if they don't get it.'

(About Titania and Oberon) 'It's power games, and sex is the first weapon they use against each other.'

The views of actors who have played fairies can help your thinking. Some people have very clear ideas about the fairies on stage. Deciding how to present the fairies is vital to how you present the play. Pick a scene from the play and produce it in a number of contrasting ways, with different kinds of fairies. This will bring out the variety of ways of looking at the fairies and the fairy world, and different ways of looking at the play itself.

After a drawing illustrating the play. Compare this with page 74.
What view of the fairies do the pictures present?

The Mechanicals' play

These comments by actors indicate how some actors think about the Mechanicals.

'The more serious the Mechanicals are about their play, the more intent and earnest, the funnier the result is. It's easy to get a bit self-indulgent when performing their play. But to them it is the most serious and terrifying thing, they're going to the palace to perform.'

'I've played so many people like that who are bigheaded or obsessive. I always try and see their problems and their point of view. Bottom's just a little fish in a little pond who puffs himself up – which is what comedy is all about.'

One of the best sections of the play to explore is the Mechanicals' play in Act 5. There are a host of possibilities here, so don't be limited by these suggestions. The whole play can be presented as it stands. Or it can be changed in a variety of ways – modern comments on the production from another audience, miming only, re-written in the language of some other sub-culture (say, an American cowboy version, and so on). Perhaps the experimental approaches could come first: miming, then some degree of cutting/re-writing, and then a 'full' production. But even when you are tackling a 'full' production, keep experimenting. Try different versions (with the Mechanicals grimly determined to do their best, frightened by the whole experience of acting in front of the court, or totally over the top). It would be useful to compare how *your* play develops with the way the Mechanicals' play develops in rehearsal.

Images

Visually, the play is one of the richest of all Shakespeare's plays, and this could lead to a variety of activities. Drawing (and creating) a set and scenery, costume design and posters for the play is an excellent way of developing your ideas, either as a group or on your own. Still photographs (or other visual presentations) of moments in a production offer another valuable means of engaging with the visual side of the play. Another good technique is the use of video, which offers a permanent record of the improvisation and performance that can be discussed (and edited). Although video takes much more time than performing to an audience, it is worthwhile exploring the play in this way.

Presenting Shakespeare's language

It's possible to create a presentation that concentrates on the language of the play. Make displays that will put across what you feel are some of the most important features of Shakespeare's language. Use the 'Watch your language' activities on pages 32, 58 and 157–163 for ideas, but include other things, such as:

- famous favourite lines from the play;
- photographs of acting activities next to the lines from the script;
- your own attempts at writing like Shakespeare;
- drawings of Shakespeare's verbal 'pictures' opposite his verse;
- examples of different kinds of wordplay and humour.

Different fonts (if you are using a computer to print) can help make your displays attractive.

Match the forms of the writing with the characters (lyrics for the fairies, prose for the Mechanicals, and so on), explaining what you think the connection is between the characters and the form. For example, in Shakespeare's time, high-status characters in plays were usually expected to speak in verse and low-status characters in prose. Experiment with the forms Shakespeare uses, writing your own blank verse, rhyming couplets, lyrics and prose. Link the kind of language to the characters and forms (the Mechanicals use working people's language in prose, the court uses upper-class language and blank verse, and so on). Write your own prose and verse this way, where the language fits the character and form.

Writing is, in part, creating images with words. Acting creates images too (but on stage). Make a display of what you feel are the key images in the play, using photographs and drawings for the acting images, and including the key images in words.

Going to see a production (or seeing a film, video or television version of the play) is essential. The main thing is to watch and enjoy the play, but you might study one key character, and then follow that character through the performance. Or you might develop your idea of the fairies and sets, and then compare them with those used in the production. Read and discuss reviews before you go, and then comment on their judgements after you've seen the production.

Young lovers and courtship

The importance of courtship and marriage in the play led many people to think *A Midsummer Night's Dream* was written as an entertainment for an aristocratic wedding, but this is almost certainly not true. But it is about love and relationships. Compare the attitudes to love and relationships in the play with attitudes among your friends, your parents and different groups in society today. Start by comparing the young lovers in the play with any you may know.

One of the ideas in the play is that there is a difference between 'doting' and 'love', something like the distinction between fancying someone (being physically attracted to them) and loving them. But the play also presents 'love' as a kind of madness, a way of looking at someone that is like magic (or, at least, irrational). These days love is often presented as an extremely good thing, but in the play 'reason and love keep little company together'. Considering different examples, think about what love means today and what it seems to mean in the play. You could then make a display – perhaps using photographs and illustrations – to show the differences (and similarities). What is your own view of love?

But of course the play revolves around the conflicts in relationships as well as love. For each relationship, identify the causes of the conflicts (even for Pyramus and Thisbe, although the Mechanicals' play unintentionally mocks their situation, just as Shakespeare seems to be mocking the lovers in his play). Explain your view of how these conflicts are resolved, and whether the characters have changed by the end of the play.

Another way of looking at this is to consider how different the relationships appear at different points in the play. For each relationship, pick a moment in the wood to act out, and then a moment from Act 4 or Act 5. Describe the feelings that seem to be dominant in these two Acts. Some people think that the wood was a place where the lovers could really display their emotions (both love *and* hate), away from the restrictions of law, society and their parents. How does this view compare with what you have found?

Patterns or structures

There are many patterns in the play. Find as many as you can. For example, there are the different relationships between the lovers (who loves who at different points – see the diagrams on pages 10, 50, 76 and 108). There are also patterns in the play as a whole to do with places, time of day (or night), characters (and stereotypes associated with different social classes), and other things, including structures, like the division of the play into five Acts. For each of the patterns you discover, write down as many features associated with the pattern as you can find.

Of course just finding a pattern isn't enough. Take the pattern of the play in terms of place (palace–wood–palace). Your list of features of this pattern could make you think the palace was associated with reason and the wood with emotion. But there is a lot of emotion in the scenes in the palace. The palace is the mortal world and the wood is the fairy world – but the fairies do appear in the palace at the end of the play. Use your list of features associated with each pattern to interpret the pattern, but don't feel there has to be just one 'right' answer.

There are other kinds of pattern you could look for:

- patterns of power (men and women, mortals and fairies, and so on);
- patterns of images (day and night, Bottom and asses, sleep and dreams, and so on);
- patterns of experiences (for example, the experience of the lovers and Bottom in the wood creates a sense of growing unreality for them and the audience);
- patterns of appearance versus reality; or conflict; or change.

Sometimes it is helpful to think of certain patterns as the 'themes' of the play (helping you answer the question 'What is the play about?'). But however you think of them, after finding as many patterns as you can and trying to interpret them, see if the patterns themselves fit together somehow. You could make charts or diagrams to show your ideas. Don't worry if you don't come to any final conclusions – perhaps there aren't any. It is exploring how the whole play is structured that matters.

Ideas in – and out of – the play

Like exploring patterns in *A Midsummer Night's Dream*, you can explore ideas related to it. In the play, 'imagination' is the mind's ability to create, or change what it perceives (especially when the person is in love). Imagination is also what creates the audience's vision – and particularly the author's.

There are other interesting ideas about the play. One is based on the many festivals in which lovers and others were allowed to do things normally forbidden (like being alone in the wood all night). Festivals (like holidays today) were a kind of release from the pressures of normal life, after which normal life seemed better, both for the society and the individual – or so the theory suggested. Another idea suggests that the fairies represent natural forces (both in the world and in the minds of the characters), as opposed to laws and reason. Using your work on patterns, discuss your own theories or ideas about what might be the play's central ideas – if any.

The trouble with theories or interpretations is they seem to answer some of the questions, but not all of them. They can be contradictory. For example, imagination is criticised in Theseus' speech in Act 5 Scene 1, lines 2–22, and mocked in the lovers' changes of partners. Yet the Mechanicals' lack of imagination is also mocked. Or Puck thinks 'what fools these mortals be', but Oberon and Titania (and Puck himself) hardly behave in a sensible way. In thinking about the play, it is possible to 'de-construct it' – but none of these ideas is necessarily valid, because they come from characters who are 'visions', 'shadows', the product of Shakespeare's and our own imagination. But thinking about these ideas – and the problems with them – can help you look at the play in new ways.

It isn't the ideas that matter most, however, it's the play itself, the performances you are in and see. It's the experience of being involved as part of an audience or part of the play. And it's the direct contact with Shakespeare himself, hearing his words and seeing his play despite the 400 years that have passed:

So, good night unto you all.
Give me your hands, if we be friends,
And Robin shall restore amends.

Looking at the language

Old language

Shakespeare's language can seem complex and difficult when you first encounter it. With time, this impression fades and you will find it easier, but Shakespeare's language always remains a challenge.

One challenge is the words that Shakespeare uses. You can look through the words and phrases explained on each left-hand page and decide for yourself how difficult these are. On closer inspection, you will find many of them are not as difficult as they seem. Take, for example, the words explained on page 124. The use of the words 'periods', 'points' and 'stop' are all to do with punctuation, and this is easy enough to understand once you read the explanation (in fact, you may well have understood it first time!). 'Capacity', in the phrase 'in my capacity', seems to have a slightly different meaning to the one it has now, though we still write about people's intellectual capacity.

* Working in small groups, divide the words explained on six left-hand pages into those that are easy to understand, perhaps with a little help, and those which seem to have no link with more modern English. Are the words which Shakespeare uses really that difficult?

One thing you may wish to consider is that, of all the major writers in English, Shakespeare uses the largest number of different words, easily more than four times as many as most authors. He also uses many different meanings of words – he obviously enjoyed playing with language.

It's often said that Shakespeare is hard to understand because the world is so different now from the world of 400 years ago. There are parts of the play where it is clear that Shakespeare's world was very different from ours:

That frights the maidens of the villagery,
Skim milk, and sometimes labour in the quern,
And bootless make the breathless housewife churn,
And sometime make the drink to bear no barm.
(Act 2 Scene 1, lines 35–8)

Here, the agricultural England of 1590 is much in evidence (most critics agree that the play was written in the 1590s). But given that the play is set in legendary Athens, not in Shakespeare's England and time, there is very little that refers directly only to Shakespeare's day.

- Make a list of some of specific examples in the play (like the four lines above) where the language seems to refer closely to the world of the 1590s and could not really apply to our own day.

- Find any passage in the play that you cannot link to modern English. Talk together about the difficulties you have with the language. You may find that the complexities are usually not some different, older language so much as very compressed 'rich' writing – which takes us to our next topic: literary language.

Literary language

Shakespeare's language isn't just old, it's literary. As Shakespeare was writing *A Midsummer Night's Dream*, he drew upon many other kinds of writing and stories: Greek and Roman mythology, all kinds of folk tales and legends, old plays, and so on. His language is also shaped and fashioned for the Elizabethan stage. Unlike some of today's film and television, Elizabethan playwrights often used complex and playful language, rather than trying to be realistic.

This is one of the many reasons that Shakespeare's language is not the same as the ordinary speech we use in daily life. The idea that people in Shakespeare's day spoke as the characters in his plays is not true (for example, they certainly did not speak in rhyme!). Why did Shakespeare not use the ordinary speech of real people? One answer is simply that he followed the stage conventions of the time, for example, in writing much of the play in verse. If you want another answer, just listen carefully to what people really say, perhaps to what you and your friends talk about. Would you like to see a play which accurately copied genuine conversations?

Of course, there are times when the language in speeches seems to run away with itself, as in Bottom's lines:

> The eye of man hath not heard, the ear of man hath not seen, man's hand is not able to taste, his tongue to conceive, nor his heart to report what my dream was!
> (Act 4 Scene 1, lines 205–7)

Transformation! Bottom and Titania in Benjamin Britten's opera
of the play. Opera versions of Shakespeare's plays cut the language very
heavily – or rewrite it.

The language matches the character: Bottom often exaggerates and muddles things up, and here, as usual, he is getting things wrong. Shakespeare could just have given him the line: 'The eye of man hath not heard what my dream was!' But Bottom goes far beyond that, adding comic statement to comic statement. In doing this, Bottom's speech also illustrates a general point about Shakespeare's language. He often uses lists: piling up item on item. If you turn to a few pages at random, you can probably find a list of some kind on each.

There are many complex lines in the play, and many speeches that are ornate and 'poetic' (for example, Titania's 'These are the forgeries of jealousy' in Act 2 Scene 1, lines 81–117). These 'poetic' qualities are strengths: they mean the play offers more than just character and plot, giving a rich store of images, ideas and language to entertain and engage the audience. Because so much Shakespeare is studied for examinations, students often try to understand everything, but this is unrealistic: what communication from anyone do we ever really fully understand?

Shakespeare's language is part of the whole fabric of the play. It creates visions of fairies, courtiers and the Mechanicals, all embodied in a language that is, in itself, part of the entertainment.

Yet, despite his own mastery of language, Shakespeare seems to make fun of himself and other poets. He does this very obviously in the Mechanicals' Pyramus and Thisbe play, mocking many of the language devices used by poets and playwrights. In Theseus' speech (Act 5 Scene 1, lines 2–22), he compares poets to lovers and madmen. And in the final speech of the play, Shakespeare claims the play itself is but a vision:

> And this weak and idle theme,
> No more yielding but a dream.
> (Act 5 Scene 1, lines 405–6)

At the same time, the characters who do not have imagination are implicitly criticised in the play. Perhaps the language that Shakespeare creates is like the play itself: imaginative, entertaining, absurd, serious, tragic, magical and ordinary. Or, to look at it another way, the play Shakespeare writes is the local habitation and a name he creates through his language:

> The poet's eye, in a fine frenzy rolling,
> Doth glance from heaven to earth, from earth to heaven;
> And as imagination bodies forth

The forms of things unknown, the poet's pen
Turns them to shapes, and gives to airy nothing
A local habitation and a name.
(Act 5 Scene 1, lines 12–17)

This raises another major issue. Shakespeare creates characters who speak, he does not speak himself. Everything in the play is seen through these characters and their words, and the patterns that are created in the play itself.

Kevin Kline as Bottom in the 1999 film of *A Midsummer Night's Dream*.
Say how this portrayal of Bottom suggests he speaks his language.

Structures of language

The language of the play has its own structures, from prose (mainly spoken by the Mechanicals) to different kinds of verse (mainly spoken by the court and the fairies). The language of the characters reflects their social position, as well as creating different kinds of comedy.

Verse patterns (or metre) are constructed from stressed and unstressed syllables. A stressed syllable is one that is given more emphasis when spoken (so it is the first syllable in 'metre' and 'syllable'). In this play, Shakespeare most often uses a metrical pattern called iambic pentameter where there is a loose pattern of unstressed (x) and stressed (/) syllables, with five stressed syllables in each line (ti-TUM ti-TUM ti-TUM ti-TUM ti-TUM):

x / x / x / x / x /
This man with lanthorn, dog, and bush of thorn

Much of this verse is in rhyme (unrhymed iambic pentameter is called blank verse). But Shakespeare also uses other metres, most obviously four-stress rhythm as in 'You spotted snakes with double tongue', and in the final 67 lines of the play.

- Try writing a modern speech that fits the verse pattern of iambic pentameter (five stresses in each line). When you write your modern speech in Shakespeare's metre, what do you notice? What does it suggest about Shakespeare?

Of course, there are other patterns that differentiate the characters. For example, examine Theseus' speeches and make a list of the qualities they have (balanced? measured? reasonable? wise? masculine? intolerant? or ...?). Then try to explain how Shakespeare uses language to create those effects. If you find it difficult at first, try comparing one of Theseus' speeches with one of Bottom's.

The language of the characters – the words, patterns and images they use – creates their characters as much as their actions or the plot. For example, in his speech to Hermia early in Act 1, Theseus' language is, at times, very manipulative, presenting being a nun through a series of negative images ('endure the livery of a nun', 'barren sister', 'faint hymns', 'cold fruitless moon'). Try examining the speeches of your favourite character in order to identify the patterns of language they use, and to what effect.

There are other things that influence how you might respond to the language. Any speech in the play is meant to be spoken by an actor, and the very appearance of that actor, how she moves, her tone of voice, the stage setting, and other factors affect how Shakespeare's language is embodied, and what impact it has on the audience. At times it can be difficult to know how to respond to Shakespeare's script. Many people find the following passage gives them problems:

LYSANDER The course of true love never did run smooth;
But either it was different in blood –
HERMIA O cross! too high to be enthralled to low.
LYSANDER Or else misgraffèd in respect of years –
HERMIA O spite! too old to be engaged to young.
LYSANDER Or else it stood upon the choice of friends –
HERMIA O hell, to choose love by another's eyes!

The first line is proverbial now, but the exclamations which follow ('O cross!' 'O spite!' 'O hell') are absurd and comical, but literary and highly patterned as well. For example, Shakespeare is using one of his favourite language structures, antithesis – setting words or phrases against each other (high/low, old/young). When these lines are spoken on stage, it can be difficult to keep the sense of characters in love, and the exaggerating, formal language dominates. Try to find one or two other moments like this in the play where the language might seem to overwhelm or contradict the emotions. What is your reaction to such moments?

So what does it all mean?

There is part of us that wants things to be simple, for there to be a straightforward answer to the question: what does this speech mean? The simplest answer to this question is that in *A Midsummer Night's Dream* speeches have different meanings at the same time. The play has been around for over 400 years and people are still debating and exploring these different meanings. This is what you are doing as you watch, read and act out the play. The complexity of the play and its language is part of the appeal of Shakespeare: it is an exploration in which there is no final, complete, and 'right' explanation. Perhaps Bottom was right:

I have had a most rare vision. I have had a dream, past the wit of man to say what dream it was.

William Shakespeare 1564–1616

1564 Born Stratford-upon-Avon, eldest son of John and Mary Shakespeare.

1582 Marries Anne Hathaway of Shottery, near Stratford.

1583 Daughter, Susanna, born.

1585 Twins, son and daughter, Hamnet and Judith, born.

1592 First mention of Shakespeare in London. Robert Greene, another playwright, described Shakespeare as 'an upstart crow beautified with our feathers ...'. Greene seems to have been jealous of Shakespeare. He mocked Shakespeare's name, calling him 'the only Shake-scene in a country' (presumably because Shakespeare was writing successful plays).

1595 A shareholder in 'The Lord Chamberlain's Men', an acting company that became extremely popular.

1596 Son Hamnet dies, aged eleven.
Father, John, granted arms (acknowledged as a gentleman).

1597 Buys New Place, the grandest house in Stratford.

1598 Acts in Ben Jonson's *Every Man in His Humour*.

1599 Globe Theatre opens on Bankside. Performances in the open air.

1601 Father, John, dies.

1603 James I grants Shakespeare's company a royal patent: 'The Lord Chamberlain's Men' became 'The King's Men' and played about twelve performances each year at court.

1607 Daughter, Susanna, marries Dr John Hall.

1608 Mother, Mary, dies.

1609 'The King's Men' begin performing indoors at Blackfriars Theatre.

1610 Probably returned from London to live in Stratford.

1616 Daughter, Judith, marries Thomas Quiney.
Dies. Buried in Holy Trinity Church, Stratford-upon-Avon.

The plays and poems
(no one knows exactly when he wrote each play)

1589–1595 *The Two Gentlemen of Verona, The Taming of the Shrew, First, Second and Third Parts of King Henry VI, Titus Andronicus, King Richard III, The Comedy of Errors, Love's Labour's Lost, A Midsummer Night's Dream, Romeo and Juliet, King Richard II* (and the long poems *Venus and Adonis* and *The Rape of Lucrece*).

1596–1599 *King John, The Merchant of Venice, First and Second Parts of King Henry IV, The Merry Wives of Windsor, Much Ado About Nothing, King Henry V, Julius Caesar* (and probably the *Sonnets*).

1600–1605 *As You Like It, Hamlet, Twelfth Night, Troilus and Cressida, Measure for Measure, Othello, All's Well That Ends Well, Timon of Athens, King Lear*.

1606–1611 *Macbeth, Antony and Cleopatra, Pericles, Coriolanus, The Winter's Tale, Cymbeline, The Tempest*.

1613 *King Henry VIII, The Two Noble Kinsmen* (both probably with John Fletcher).

1623 Shakespeare's plays published as a collection (now called the First Folio).